Home
inspired by *Love* and *Beauty*

Dear Reader,

Inspired homes can change lives. Like a complex tapestry, home is crafted tenderly stitch-by-stitch and so interlaced that it's hard to pull one strand without others being drawn along. This book tells the story of the tapestry of home and all its potential. It explores how your relationship to your home can be one of friendship—a quiet partner that weaves together your inner private world, family, friends, a physical place, treasured things, sacred values, gardens, as well as your neighborhood, city, nation, nature, and planet creating your unique place in the world. May your home be showered with grace, meaning, and happiness.

Margaret Lulic

Home *inspired by* Love *and* Beauty

Margaret A. Lulic, MA

Blue Edge Publishing
Minneapolis

Published by
Blue Edge Publishing
www.lulicbooks.com

Cover photos by Michael Fitzgerald, FitzgeraldPhotography.com
Original illustrations by Lara Crombie
Book design by Dorie McClelland, Spring Book Design

ISBN: 978-0-9828374-0-5

The stories told here are of several types. Some are my families. Others are from friends, clients, and associates used with permission. Others are composite stories that I have heard, read about, or supplemented to explain an idea. In all cases, I have tried to respect individual privacy.

In Gratitude
Mary and Thomas Lulic
Mary and Joseph Reid
Lee and Joseph Timpane

As I was writing this book, Aunt Mary, one of my special elders, died. As we deal with the latter years of our parents' lives and their deaths, we not only recognize their enormous impact on our lives, but we also step forward to take our turn as the elders. What lessons have we learned, and what will we pass on? From all my parents, I experienced how love, not wealth, created a meaningful home, and beauty had an integrity that touched every aspect of the home.

From my parents, Mary and Tom Lulic, I learned that people could love each other deeply and create a home despite a large gap in age and culture. My mother was a Minnesota farm girl, and my dad was a post World War I immigrant from Croatia. My grandparents' understanding of the world was that if you weren't Irish Catholic, you weren't really Catholic. A marriage to my Croatian Catholic father was like marrying outside the church, and my mother was disowned for a time. Eventually, my parents overcame that disapproval and discrimination. I was young when they died, so I had a second experience of home.

My Aunt Mary and Uncle Joe took me into their large family, even though, they were already working hard to make ends meet and care for my seven cousins. Uncle Joe brought me home, sandwiching me into their small house. My aunt truly believed that cleanliness and neatness were next to godliness; that was the material way you made a lovely home. There was a more significant lesson that always astonished me. At holidays and other special occasions, that small home magically expanded to accommodate additional relatives and friends. There was also a welcoming place at the table for my oldest cousins' college friends regardless of race, country of origin, or ethnicity. When our daughter was born, my mothering aunt became a loving grandmother. Legal blood ties are less important than heart ties in a home.

When Bob and I were married, I was blessed with another mom and dad. Small tight families have a different challenge opening their hearts and homes to someone new; my in-laws certainly rose to the occasion. They grew up in the Depression and met in the armed services during World War II. That contributed to a work-hard-and-save philosophy leading to self-sufficiency and independence. Complementing this was a wonderful sense of humor and generosity. Christmas (with Mom's bargain hunting skills) made us believe there was a Santa Claus. Dad believed you should work hard, and serve your country and customers honestly and loyally. Mom had two love affairs with beauty. She loved cut glass, so Dad pampered her with many pieces. The first time I went to their home, I saw more cut glass vases and bowls than I had seen in my whole life. Her second love was flowers. Her loving touch could make a bouquet of flowers last longer than anyone I have ever known.

Contents

Acknowledgments

My husband, Bob, and my daughter and son-in-law, Laura and Joe, have my love and gratitude for their support and willingness to share some of our stories. Our extended family and friends have contributed to our lives and understanding of home. We love and cherish them. We also appreciate the wise advisors who helped us create our home over the decades.

Special thanks to BJ Anderson, Susan Anderson, Mary Brown, Margaret Reid Carter, Sally Deke, Teresa Hanstad, Carole Hyder, and Cindy Kelley for their valuable feedback on the book early in this process. It is a different book because of them.

I am indebted to all the people whose stories have touched me and found their way into this book through diverse paths. The stories say so much more than just writing about ideas.

I have been blessed with talented and delightful experts who have shared this journey. Without my writing partner, Carole Hyder, I'm not sure if I would have started this book. Dorrine Turecamo inspired me to keep going through the final drafts. Dorie McClelland provided a beautiful cover and book design. Michael Fitzgerald's photography and Lara Crombie's drawings provide a lovely visual complement to the written text. Linda White provided helpful insights on marketing.

Home
inspired by *Love and Beauty*

Conceived in Love

Today, homes are great treasures for far more people than ever before in history, but the meaning of home has changed considerably over the centuries. We don't notice that since we have no basis for comparison. The experience is similar to that raised with the question, "Does a fish know its home is water?" We are as immersed in what is familiar to us as the fish is. Looking back in time or through a different worldview can help us break away from the familiar and open up discoveries.

Imagine if you could slip into a 14th century European house on a typical day. What would you see that would surprise you? It might be the sheer number of people in a single household. At first, it seems you have appeared at a party or meeting. The average household consists of up to twenty-five people, many of whom are not related. In addition to the family, there are the servants, employees, apprentices, friends, and relatives.

Next, you might notice much of the activity is taking place in one great hall. It resembles today's great room or family room, except this room is oriented to the street. There is the clamor of people engaging in different activities in one space. Some are clearly active in the business of the household as an artisan or shopkeeper. Others are cooking, eating, chopping, bartering, playing, or sleeping.

The structure, furnishings, and decorations are minimal. Furniture serves utilitarian purposes, often with more than one function. The chest serves as a place for storage, sitting, standing, sleeping, and writing. The furniture seems to move around all day serving different purposes. Neither table nor chair has a place of its own. Since these items lack meaning, they are treated thoughtlessly.

The house is a shelter for working and living in a very communal and public way. Privacy doesn't seem to exist in the mind or behavior of the occupants. Home, as we know it, did not exist, but the first hints of the Renaissance are just around the corner and with it the next step in a long journey toward creating a loving home.

By the latter part of the 20th century, the new field of environmental psychology, the science of place, asserts that your behavior and the places within which it occurs are an integrated unit. Describing one without the other is capturing only part of the picture. Winifred Gallagher, author of *The Power of Place* and *House Thinking*, would explain that "Not unlike medicines, places have effects, and that when accurately 'prescribed,' they can make us feel better." Our homes have tremendous potential to nurture and heal us, to help us grow, and to surround us as well as those we love with beauty and harmony.

Clare Cooper Marcus, in her book, *House as a Mirror of Self,* points out that part of our human development involves meaningful relationships with significant physical environments as well as with people. Home has not received enough attention because all the typical fields of study slice and dice the world in ways that do not take into account one of our greatest emotional connections—our home. Welcome to a journey into this world where we will draw on insights from many fields but, most importantly, from people who love their homes.

Welcome Home
A loving home is the unity of a specific dwelling, all those people and things that it shelters, and the sense of treasuring and being treasured. In its fullest form, everything about the home has been conceived in love and inspired by beauty—not just the physical aspects—but the relationships, values, and daily rituals. The result is the happiness, which Aristotle argues is the deepest desire of humanity. This is not just the happiness of pleasure or peace of mind; it is the happiness of participation in something meaningful. The act of conceiving arises from your inner life of imagination, understanding, and creativity. It pervades every aspect of your special place and your interaction with it, starting with your arrival home.

When do you feel you have returned home? Is it as you see your familiar site from the street corner or pull into your driveway? Is it as you open the back door, fold your arms around a loved one, or sink into your favorite chair? Perhaps the answer changes with circumstances. I have different moments that ring the bell of my heart and announce, "I'm home."

One moment is as I reach the intersection where I live and remember the first time I saw my house. In spring, summer, and fall, the moment that takes precedence comes as I open the gate to walk through my gardens. They bring a smile to my face. In winter or rainy weather, it is when I open my warm honey-oak stained back door. Before our dog died, it was Katie's joyous dash and bark as she beat everyone else in greeting me. A home welcomes us in so many different ways.

The doors that greet us matter. Metaphorically, doors may be signs of danger or safety, openings and closings to life, privacy, or concealment. Your doors send signals to you and to others. The front door welcomes a diverse set of people—visitors, delivery people, mail and news carriers, neighborhood connections, politicians running for election, and solicitors.

One week was particularly busy for us with the latter: Girl Scout cookies were delivered, the National Honor Society at the local high school collected for the food shelves, and there were three non-profits who came by asking for donations or for us to sign petitions for local, national, and global issues.

I mentioned this to the last person who came, and his answering comment caught my attention. He said that the canvassing coordinators must have made a mistake. As I asked more questions, I discovered that my neighborhood is the second most canvassed community in the United States because we tend to be active, involved, and contribute. I hadn't thought about how important front doors are in embracing the world.

At the time, we were considering replacing both of our old exterior doors with oak, prairie-style, doors that matched the integrity of the design of our home. That decision required extra time to find the right doors and would be more expensive than a basic functional door. In particular, we were debating about the extra cost for the back door. It already had a cheaper door than the front entrance.

In reading Sarah Susanka's book, *The Not So Big House,* there were some good questions that helped us think about this issue. Sarah is a former client and a friend. She asked, "But why do we relegate ourselves secondary status when it comes to the way we enter our houses?" That was a good question. Since we always park in the garage or driveway, we come home through the back kitchen door. We decided to delight ourselves with the prairie-style doors for both entrances, so we would have the same experience guests have at the front door.

Sometime later a funny thing happened. It was late September, and I was sorting through a pile of old Southwest Journals, our excellent neighborhood newspaper. My things-to-be-read pile was getting large. While culling the pile down, I turned one of these newspapers over, and something leaped off the page at me. It was a photo of our front door along with seven other front doors. The article was called, "Make An Entrance: What does your front door say about you?" My home had been chosen as having a welcoming entrance. Strangers had noticed our caring touch.

Every sense you or your guests have can be touched when those doors open. Lights are welcoming. They suggest warmth and a friendly feeling. Someone or something is waiting for you. Even if you live alone, you can put a light on a timer or have motion sensitive lights installed. The colors you see as you follow a path into the home can delight your eyes. Textures and fabrics don't even have to touch us physically to work their magic. Scents coming from the kitchen or a bouquet of flowers seep into hearts, not just noses, triggering memories. The sounds of home are uniquely yours. Hopefully, they are soothing or happy sounds most of the time.

Alex is sensitive to color and has repainted his entry four times to get it just right. Wendy's back door opens into her kitchen. There is no mudroom. The cascade of shoes and jackets on the hooks and shelves by the entry constantly irritated her. With a limited budget, she felt stuck. She couldn't afford to have a cabinet built. She found a simple and appealing solution using a curtain that blended with the walls. The mess evaporated, replaced with softness.

Marie and Jim both worked outside their home, so they had a ritual for coming home. They checked weekly schedules to determine which nights they could make it work. Whoever was home first started dinner and developed a plan for the children. After the other parent had arrived home and greeted the children, they were sent off to bedrooms to do homework or outside to play or to the family room for a show. Then Marie and Jim settled down in the living room with a glass of wine for a minimum of twenty minutes of conversation.

For those who share their home with family or friends—both the two-legged and four-legged—words, hugs, kisses, eye connections, and ruffled heads make us sigh in peace. You anticipate an evening that will refresh and renew you. This is one way to come home. What is your way? What do you want it to be? Make one simple adjustment like those described above that will bring a smile to your face each night. Your home will cooperate.

Architects propose that we want more than shelter from buildings, especially our homes; we want them to speak to us of that which is important—feelings, values, our most deeply held aspirations. Alain de Botton, in *The Architecture of Happiness*, says that when we return home, "We can slowly resume contact with a more authentic self, who was there waiting in the wings for us to end our performance. . . . The materials around us will speak to us of the highest hopes we have for ourselves. In this setting we come close to a state of mind marked by integrity and vitality. We can, in a profound sense, return home."

Longing for Home

The more work, technology, and troubling local and global issues invade our lives, the more we seek shelter and something uplifting. We yearn for meaning in our lives. People look in many places and try doing many things. Wonderful opportunities wait for us where we live and among those with whom we share our lives. Creating a meaningful home is the work and joy of a lifetime.

This book is intended to be your companion if you

are on a journey to create a home that is welcoming, warm, renewing, and ready to nurture and inspire you. The word home includes all those places we live—house, duplex, condominium, apartment, or mobile home. Ownership isn't a requirement to feel at home.

One other clarification—in this book, home is not the same as family. If the two words were identical, that would suggest that living alone or without children disqualifies you from having a home. Family may be an integral part of home for some but not for others. Economic booms allow more single people to have their own places. Economic downturns tend to reduce the number of households but increase their size. So who is in the household may change, but the desire for a home, regardless of where that is or how many live together, remains.

According to French philosopher and mystic, Simone Weil, "To be rooted is perhaps the most important and least recognized need of the human soul." Our families and homes are the most likely places for us to develop these roots. They are the soil, and we are the plants. The soil needs to be cultivated, weeded, and nourished or the soil cannot sustain the plant. Being rooted or not will affect all aspects of our health and well-being.

You aren't alone if you are investing more time and energy in family, home, and meaning. Market researchers have names such as cocooning and nesting and experiential to describe a change in behavior in recent years. The research reports an increased desire to focus on these meaningful aspects of our lives.

Other experts have also added insight to the phenomenon of home. In *The Cultural Creatives,* authors Paul Ray and Sherry Anderson describe the values and ideals that are emerging around lifestyles, home, and cultural issues. The findings of these publications are consistent with the list I have developed in the following exercise.

These items in the next exercise represent what I hear from family, friends, clients, and readers when asked to contrast houses and homes. The distinctions make a world of difference. You could check which contrasts matter to you. Also consider if you might have additional ideas. Not everyone wants a home. There is nothing wrong with wanting a house if it is the right answer for you. I've desired both but at different stages of life.

The lists are not necessarily incompatible. Another way to frame it could be to ask to what degree do you want each of these items? Some of the pairings suggest a continuum rather than a choice. Oasis from the storms of life easily begins with shelter from the elements and develops beyond it. Part of the difference lies in how much of which column you want. It may also vary depending on point-of-view; each member of the household may experience something different.

You might want to have others in your household complete the exercise. Then you can compare and search for insights, not for who is right or wrong.

Exercise

Select which items are most important or most accurate for you.

HOUSE	HOME
Place to live	Place of love
A place to reside	A place to come to life
Shelter from elements	Oasis from the storms of life
Place to eat and sleep	Place to nourish my family or me in all areas of life
Store/display/use my stuff	Full of stories and memories
Show who I am	Discover who I'm becoming
Costs me money	Investment in self/family
Provides privacy	Provides peace and quiet
Place to entertain	Place to engage in meaningful relationships w/all life
Feels cool	Feels warm
Invites browsing	Invites sitting and discussion
Focus on tangibles	Focus on meaning
Displays success	Defines purpose
Belongs to me	Mutual belonging
Efficient	Effective
Right choices	Right questions
Fast	Paced
A revolving door	A place to enjoy time
A jumping-off point	A journey
Decorate to make lovely	Decorate for warmth/meaning

Defining what house and home mean to you and to your significant others builds understanding, clarity, insight, and inspiration. This is true whether you are renting, buying, remodeling, decorating, maintaining, or cleaning. It increases the probability that you and your family will be content, healthy, and happy.

The longing for home is about a desire to love and be loved, not only with people, but also with a place and cherished things. It is also about belonging. Somewhere in this immense universe you want a little corner that is safe, secure, and yours. You want a touch of magic combined with true blue loyalty.

Home is the place you most expect to feel an unbreakable bond; I am yours and you are mine. That intense emotional connection happens between people and between people and their pets. It can also manifest with places and cherished things. It may be between the owner and the home itself. Perhaps these are fundamental needs buried in your genetic memory or an integral part of your emotional limbic brain. That's why it hurts so much when you lose it or are deprived of it.

The first element in a definition of home is that it's conceived in love. That is why for many people, home is about their family, not a place. When we have traveled in Mexico and Greece, we have noticed that the plaza seemed more like home in those countries than houses did. I asked a Hispanic and Greek friend about that. As in all cultures and socio-economic groups the answers will vary to some degree, but they felt that on the whole my observation was true.

Many families go to the plaza almost every night after dinner. It is like one extremely large family room for a whole neighborhood. The extended family, friends, and neighbors are all there with every generation intermingling. The children play and the adults talk, laugh, sing, tell stories, and even dance. Activities don't have to be planned; they happen spontaneously. People matter, not the house.

There is variation in the United States as well, but on the whole, there is a greater emphasis on the place called home. The people and the place that raised you have influenced your understanding of house and home. Hopefully, they modeled a home conceived in love regardless of whether home meant people, or people and a house. That doesn't mean you have to do it the same way. It just means that you have the experience buried within you to bring to your home-making efforts. If love was not pervasive in your childhood, then you and your home have the opportunity to engage in a discovery process that allows you to overcome the deficiencies of the past and to build new dreams.

Fast Backward

Our personal life stories influence the values, attitudes, experiences, and preferences we bring to our relationships with our dwellings. Sharing your childhood memories with others illuminates all aspects of house and home. It helps explain why one person wants a rambler in the suburbs, and the other wants a 1920s Arts and Crafts home in the city. You begin to understand why you love different things than someone else.

One woman, responding to my on-line survey wrote, "My husband and I each took your survey about homes and meaningful rooms. We were surprised at how often we had chosen the same favorite room but for totally different reasons. We learned something new about each other from our home."

Recalling and sharing stories of your childhood home is more than just a journey down memory lane. It is a rediscovery of part of who you are and from where you came. Homes have sad stories to tell as well as happy ones. Tell both kinds of stories. Sadness has its own gifts of truth and beauty. I'll provide a sample by sharing my story with you.

Today, I live about a half an hour away from my childhood home. It is also a lifetime away. I occasionally drive through my former working class suburb. The first time I did this as an adult, I had been away for 15 years and discovered surprises about my old haunts. As a child, it had seemed as though they were much further apart. I could have sworn it was miles to the swimming pool, but it was less than one mile on my odometer. When I reached my former home, I was struck by how small it was. It used to seem larger.

I pulled over as memories filled me about the interior of that first home. While smaller than my current home and only a one-story house, the flow of the whole space felt right, as does the flow of my current home. The interior woodwork was darker than mine but warm and familiar as was the wood arch opening from the living room to the dining room. There was a hutch for the better dishes with a glass and wood framed door similar to our two corner hutches.

I loved the front porch and vividly remember how the two rooms adjoining it had windows that I could climb in and out of to get to the porch. One was in the living room and the other was in my bedroom. It was magical and adventurous since I could appear, disappear, and amaze my parents. Moreover, watching the neighbors through the many porch windows entertained me.

The porch taught me about play, having an interest in the neighbors, and taking care of a home. Maybe that is why I miss having a porch on my current home. An early memory is of my mom on her hands and knees painting the porch floor when I was about five-years-old. Maybe I had some little paint set of my own, but it was nothing like what my mom was doing. Her big brush spread that soft, warm, creamy, gray over the old scarred floorboards. I was amazed at the transformation and continue to have a similar experience every time a paintbrush is in my hand.

I wanted to help, but she didn't seem thrilled with my offer. My dad was not in good health, so he was only watching and keeping my mom company. He saw, not just my disappointment, but also my need to be part of this. He encouraged my mom to let me give it a try and took charge of instructing me. I felt the thrill of doing something so grownup and the pleasure of looking at it afterward. I was always careful to not scuff that floor. Children need to do meaningful work.

Despite how hard my mother worked at the canning

factory and how busy she was caring for my dad and me, she still loved her garden. She taught me about flowers, strawberries, and carrots. She had a special way of taking two hollyhock flowers and using a toothpick to create a princess. She was happy when she was gardening, and we had good times together.

Home for children is very connected to where their parents are. That was true for me, but the house/home was perhaps more important than is typical. My mom was forty-one, and my dad was sixty-four when I was born. I was a surprise baby, appearing after they had given up hope. My mom worked, my dad raised me, and we lived on modest means.

As Dad's health deteriorated, I took care of him and our home as much as he took care of me. My Aunt Mary tells of discovering me at the age of five, standing on a stool, stirring chicken noodle soup for our lunch, my skirt and crinoline slip inches from the flame. My stage of playing house was real. Our time as a family was brief because my dad died shortly after I turned seven. When I was eight-and-a-half, I found my mom dead from a burst appendix.

Kind relatives welcomed me into their home. I still felt homeless, though, through no one's fault. I had lost my parents. I had no siblings. My relatives had seven children in a small house; there was no room for my cat and dog. My house was gone and almost everything in it. In addition, my friends, neighbors, school, and everything of my familiar world were gone. I had lost my home in every way imaginable, but I couldn't have articulated that at the time.

My relatives' garage had a narrow band of land on the north side of it with a row of lilac bushes as a border. The adjoining neighbor's yard had a long row of poplars that rustled in the breeze. Hidden away in this space, I spent a lot of time in my little house in the bushes. I decorated it with sticks, colorful leaves, and pretty rocks. I nestled in this getaway thinking, sometimes crying, and other times imagining a new life. Books became my friends, and I read every possible moment in my hideout. I was building a new home inside myself.

Somewhere in all of that life experience, I developed a hunger for a home, not just a house. I learned some of my first lessons in how to create a home in the world and how many elements were necessary to create a whole. Perhaps what I lost in leaving my first home was not permanently lost, but it was seeded inside me, waiting for the right time to germinate.

Alternatives for Learning from Your Childhood Home

• Write your childhood story as if you were telling it to someone else.

• If you don't like to write, just make a list of key details.

• Tell the stories verbally.

• Consider key elements to explore including the location, physical characteristics of the places, where you spent the most time, what you loved or disliked, and what was meaningful.

• Allow aspects unique to you to dominate the story.

• Explore the story for insights about who you are

today, as well as the child you were, and your current or desired home.

• Compare your stories with others.

Searching for Home

Home seekers are very intentional in their selection of a house or home. They set parameters that include location, schools, stores, neighborhoods, nature, and distance from work and extended family. Priorities are listed in detail about house issues including size, kinds of rooms, garages, style of house, amount of light, and yards. I wonder, though, do homes have a preference for *their* companions?

In her book, *Conversations with Your Home,* Carole Hyder describes the relationship between a house and its owners. She says, "A house has a way of luring in the 'right' people at the right time . . . there is a very important reason the two have come together." She shares many stories about homes that helped heal their companion, confronted them with unresolved issues, or offered new growth opportunities.

The matching process between a home and a potential owner has as much heart magic to it as it does tangible practical requirements. In some ways, the house search is like dating, falling in love, and committing to a long-term relationship. It is in the nature of a house to be a match for certain people, but not for others. Some houses just are not equipped for an elderly person or for a large family with teens. These are concrete matching issues but others are intangible. It may be how the dwelling feels to you or whether you can see yourself happy in it. It is as if there is a subtle communication going on as the house reveals itself to you.

Perhaps you have heard stories about how someone found their home, loft, or apartment that has a magic element to it. You may have experienced it yourself or dream of doing so. The stories are diverse except for a common statement. "We (I) knew it was meant for us the moment we saw it." It is love at first sight. At times, it is as if a lightning bolt hits you; other times it is quieter and subtle, but it is there. For those who build a new house, this occurs as part of the design process or perhaps while building. It's the moment when you see the design and model and say, "That's it!"

My husband, Bob, and I started looking for a house in the late 1970s after renting a duplex for the first two years of our marriage. We had many discussions about our dreams. The house list included the typical things like those mentioned above. As we considered what mattered, values began to surface about what "home" meant. A significant insight was that we wanted a sustainable home. That meant our home could accommodate changes in our lives. It had to be small enough that two people wouldn't feel lost in it but large enough for a family.

My dream was a modest 1920s two-story house with lots of wood and windows. There were several political districts that were among my top choices of neighborhoods. Our real estate agent raised an eyebrow, looked at me, and said with some incredulity, "Are you sure political orientation is high in the priority list?" Bob preferred

a rambler. His top concerns, though, were a low maintenance exterior, a two-car garage, and a basement that had
usable space for a rec room; in other words, no octopus
furnace in the middle of the room.

At a conscious level these were house requirements,
but at an unconscious level, they spoke to what home felt
like from our youth. I had lived in a modest 1920s two-
story house during my teen years. I would feel at home in
a neighborhood that shared some values. Bob grew up in
a rambler that his parents had built. One of his favorite
rooms had been a finished basement with a pool table.

We wanted to live in the city near water. In Minneapolis, the City of Lakes, this preference isn't too hard. That
could appear to be a house-related requirement, but for
us, it also spoke to where we most felt like a couple. As
college students, we had both attended Marquette University in Milwaukee. We had strolls along nearby Lake
Michigan during our brief two-week courtship before
graduation. Bob returned to Minneapolis and an engi-
neering job while I was completing a Master's degree at
the University of Chicago. Visits to either city included
conversations by a lake.

One weekend Bob was unavailable, so our agent and
I were looking at houses. I wasn't excited by anything I
saw and was driving home feeling despondent. Out of
the blue, I had the urge to take a different route. It mean-
dered through one of the political districts I liked and had
mapped out for a door-knocking campaign in previous
elections. Three blocks to the north was a lake and two
blocks south was a creek.

It was a gloomy day. When it started to rain, I stopped looking and headed home. Coming to a four-way stop, I looked left and right to check traffic. In that glance, I saw the house on the northeast corner had a "For Sale" sign in the yard. As I cruised by, it was almost as if the house called, "Look at me!" When I did, a voice inside of me yelled, "That's my house." It was a 1920s four-square house with some Prairie and Arts and Crafts elements.

I drove around the block returning to the intersection. Mentally checking off our list, I drove up and down the street. Then I went down the alley and looked at the house from the back. It even had a two-car garage that faced the street, not the alley—just what Bob wanted but was hard to find in a house of that age. I pulled over, tore out paper, found a pen, and drew a quick sketch for Bob. This was long before the Internet brought housing information to your fingertips. I was sure it had everything, even though I couldn't see inside. I didn't know the asking price, but I could hope.

I raced home on a mission. Bob was excited by my description and drawing. We called our real estate agent. I gushed, "I found our house. Here's the address. Why didn't you show it to us? Is it out of our price range?" She was pretty sure the list price was more than we wanted to spend but promised to check. We started praying.

When she called back, she said, "I have bad news and

maybe a possibility." We gulped. "The house is over your budget; however, it has been on the market for quite a while, maybe there is negotiating room. Let me talk to their agent and see what I can learn."

She called the next afternoon. "Good news," she greeted me. "Not only has the house been on the market, but the owners have already bought a new house and are making two monthly mortgage payments. If we can visit the house tonight and make a fast offer, we might be able to negotiate a reduction and close this deal. There is someone else returning for a second visit. You're going to have to go into your backup plan and raise your limit if you want this house."

Later, as we started walking up to the house, I noticed little things I hadn't seen from my car. The house was adequately maintained, but the blue gray stucco looked somewhat sad. The shrubs were scraggly. The grass had a lot of weeds. White aluminum covered the window trim and wide house overhangs. "Good," Bob commented, "low maintenance."

The inside layout was delightful. The woodwork was the most perfect golden oak, and there was a ton of it. It had coving around the ceilings, wainscoting in the dining room, french doors leading into a small sunroom, and I was sure there were oak floors under the carpets. A good-sized kitchen with an eating area finished off the first floor. The house had great bones and structure.

We liked the four bedrooms. The master bedroom was a nice size. Two bedrooms were good sizes for children or a guest room. The fourth was being used as a bedroom, but it was more like a solarium with six windows on three walls. I could picture it as a library for my many books or an office or a den.

Up close there were flaws like all houses, but so much was right. Under the flaws, I felt this house had the character and warmth that I craved and associated with older homes. I could see what it could be. As we drove away, this place had already entered my heart and spirit and claimed me. Bob was happy with the house and with the two-car garage. He saw potential in the play-room in the basement.

It worked out just as our real estate agent had strat-egized. We found common ground. The owners came down $4000, and we went up $4000 above our preferred top number. We were going to be moving into a home that reflected our values and could support our dreams. We were ready for a long-term commitment.

Where Was the Magic?

• Use a process similar to the exercise about your child-hood home.

• Remember and share your experience if you have had one like this.

• Explore whether you have had this kind of experience in some other area of your life other than a house.

• Renew your relationship with your home. The longer you have been in your house, the more important this is. Has your abode lived up to your expectations? Exceeded them?

• Renew your acquaintance with yourself as well. What

do your priorities tell you about yourself? Have you cared for your home the way it needs? Have you grown?

Beware Remorse if Your Home Owns You

Falling in love can have pitfalls in a relationship and in a house or home. If you aren't clear about what comes first in your life and committed to that, above the magic of the moment, you can make life-changing mistakes. Money is among the top causes of divorce in marriages and home ownership.

One of the best ways to mar your joy in your house or home is for it to end-up owning you. Then it is no longer your friend. I've coached clients who feel trapped in a job or a career that is not fulfilling or even harmful to them. Many years ago, I had my first client whose story brought this issue to the forefront. Aaron had a high level position in a financial institution and the salary to match. He was in his mid-forties and unfulfilled by his work. He was worried about how his stress was affecting his marriage, his daughter, and his health. The question we explored was, "What would you do if you didn't have any constraints?"

He lit up as he answered. His heart was in music, and he had talent in that area. As we explored all options, there was an obvious pattern emerging. He couldn't pursue anything because of financial issues. Knowing that his spouse also worked, I finally asked the big question. "You have listed many options that would bring you so much more happiness, but you say you can't afford to do any of them. How can that be?" His answer was simple and straightforward. "My mortgage."

"So, are you telling me that your house owns you?" I asked. There was a long silence, very long. Shock and struggle showed all over his face. Finally, he replied, "That is a remarkably clear way of looking at the situation." He isn't alone. There are many variations on the story but the same huge roadblock.

This can happen in two ways. The first is the size of the mortgage is too large. Second, the amount of time you invest in projects on the house shifts in balance from joy to burden. In the case of someone who is renting, it can be that the rent is too high, or the environment of noisy neighbors, or safety problem takes a toll on your life, but you feel like you can't move.

There have been some key cultural drivers for many decades that contribute to boxing people into this corner. Beliefs can lead us astray. Here are a few: buy a house as an investment; until you buy one you haven't achieved the American dream; or, your house should demonstrate your success. Out of these beliefs arises a cultural rule of thumb that you should buy as much house as you can qualify for with the lender. We were advised of that in the 1970s when we were buying a home.

Our real estate agent, Eileen, was busy doing an analysis of how much house we could afford. Simultaneously, Bob and I were having a different discussion about the role of a mortgage in our life and values. Eileen's assessment said we could afford a more expensive house than the budget range we had set. When we questioned her strategy, her next immediate assumption was that we wanted to follow the secondary path—buy a starter home, build equity, sell, and move into something larger.

That was not a fit for us, either. I'm not criticizing this agent. She did a good job for us. Her thinking mirrored the normal approach. We were abnormal.

The conversation with Eileen was very helpful because it made us think more deeply about what mattered. A house can be an investment, and we would be happy to have it appreciate in value. We, however, didn't want to build our lives around that strategy. Nor did we want to take the route of buy, build equity, sell, and buy something bigger. Somehow, that felt like we would be temporary lodgers, not homeowners. The other approach isn't wrong. It could be perfect for someone else, just not us.

We agreed we didn't want a larger loan. Ideally, we wanted a smaller mortgage that we could pay off as early as possible. One financial advisor said that was unwise; it was better to have the mortgage deduction. Again, after discussion, we came to the conclusion that all the advice we were receiving was, in our case, putting the cart before the horse.

Before making any big financial commitment, thoughtful people consider what matters to them and how the financial commitment could affect the other aspects of their lives. Fewer people give serious thought to how much more they will have to spend to make the house what they want. More importantly, not enough consideration may go into assessing how the commitment could affect them if their life conditions change. It seems to be part of our human nature that we don't really believe that we will get sick, lose a job, or get divorced. Adults commiserate with each other about the foibles of youth who act as if they are invincible. Smart responsible adults have their own blind spots, especially if they fall in love with a house.

In the book *The Prophet,* Lebanese-American poet, Kahlil Gibran, speaks about home. He asks if homes have peace, remembrances, and beauty. Then he issues a warning, "Or have you only comfort, and the lust for comfort, that stealthy thing that enters the house a guest, and then becomes a host, and then a master?" He advises, "Your house shall not be an anchor but a mast." A house that owns you is an anchor; a home that supports you in your dreams is a mast.

How to Check Yourself

Take notes about the following issues.

- Imagine three scenarios that could significantly affect your income.
- Estimate a budget for other pending expenditures beyond your normal expenses for the next five years.
- Assess how long you could manage your mortgage payments if any of these scenarios occurred. Factor in what other expenses you could adjust.
- Prioritize three things that you value that could be compromised by a large mortgage, such as freedom to quit a job or make a career change if you were unhappy.
- Set a goal for the necessary level of available cash reserves that helps you feel secure.
- Discuss the implications of all this data and make confident decisions.
- Brainstorm other contingency plans or tradeoffs.

Troubled Waters

The main reasons marriages struggle are often the same reasons we struggle with our relationships with our homes. Life flows along. What at one point was all you wished for, at another point becomes something you no longer want. New needs emerge. That happens in relationships, jobs, and homes.

Sometimes the right move is to say goodbye to your home and move on. Todd and Maureen wanted to move back to Georgia before their children reached school age; they wanted to be near their extended families. One definition of home—birthplace—was of a higher priority than the physical home they had built. Everyone was thrilled with the move.

Frequently people determine they have outgrown their house. Maybe promotions and job changes have led to greater wealth and a desire for a more lovely home. Visiting too many sites during the annual ritual of new housing promotions may have whetted your appetite for something different.

Dissatisfaction has replaced satisfaction. Love for your place falters. You may want to sell your home. The dissatisfaction may be partial, so you want to remodel, not move. Either way—moving or remodeling—will be a big decision. If the individuals involved disagree, that makes it even more challenging.

This sense of dis-ease can manifest more subtly as well. Joanne did not want to move or remodel. She realized she had become too familiar with what she had. The magic was gone. Boredom and complacency had set in. She was so busy with other areas of her life, she hadn't noticed that things were a little tarnished, cracked, or peeling. When she did notice, she dismissed it. "I'll have to get to that some day." In hindsight, she saw that she had not physically moved out but emotionally had moved on.

Unless your concerns are concrete, such as a move to be near family or necessitated by a job change, there may be other options. The more you have loved your home; the more it might be worth a second effort to fall back in love. There was a time when I was ready to divorce my home—not my husband.

After twenty years in our home, I suddenly had the same energy to find a new house, as I had had to find this one. We had invested in a new roof, furnace, air conditioner, and painted every room over those years. We were about to repeat all of that effort, and I had no interest. I was bored and had functional concerns as well. A burning urge to move appeared in my life.

Bob who was usually open-minded and willing to meet me part way, was adamantly opposed. So we were struggling with the issue on and off for quite some time. It was like navigating between Scylla and Charybdis. He was Scylla, the rock, determined not to budge. I was the whirlpool, Charybdis, swirling around all the reasons to go. Issues of home and money are high on the list of sources of friction in marriages. In our ideal image, home would foster a better marriage, but sometimes house issues become the source of problems.

I ran into a former neighbor. Chris and her husband, George, had built a new home in the suburbs and moved. Our daughters had been friends, so most of Chris' and my conversations had been about our kids and homes. We had lost touch when they moved. We decided to catch up at the local coffee shop. I asked about their new house and she responded enthusiastically.

I shared my desire to move and told her the story of my frustration. Her eyes began to glisten, and she fell silent. I was baffled as to why she looked so sad. Finally, she shared the dark side of their move. Chris said George was the most adamant one in their family about moving. She was excited about building a new house, but she was also attached to her home and neighborhood in the city and had mixed feelings about leaving. As parents, they felt that the suburban schools would be better for their daughter and son. Their children, Rachelle and Will, were opposed to the move.

George traveled regularly for work leaving much of the burden for overseeing the building and moving process to Chris. She had not anticipated how stressful it would be. The number of choices and decisions to be made overwhelmed her. They fought regularly and breathed a sign of relief when the house was done. They celebrated despite their kids' reservations. They were sure they would be happy once they were settled in their new home with their own things. They assured the children that old friends could come to visit.

The move brought new surprises, she explained. Most of their furniture seemed too small in the new larger rooms. Now there were more choices to be made about window treatments and the yard. Rachelle was not happy. She wanted her old bedroom back. She didn't like the new school and the kids. The occasional visits from her old friends were not at all like being able to run down the block after school to play. She cried herself to sleep every night for weeks. Will got on the soccer team and his transition was easier.

She ended her story, "We've all adjusted. It has worked out, and the house is gorgeous. Despite that, I still have mixed feelings about the move. I really miss our old home; it had something this house may never have. Rachelle and I miss the neighborhood and friendships."

I thought about her story that night. Every partnership has its challenging times when one person's dreams are contrary to the other person's. It's one thing to have conflicts over which person takes the garbage out or how high or low to set the thermostat. It is a whole different dimension to have conflicts over dreams.

When you reach an impasse like this one, I've learned it is time to dig deeper into your urge, and find your own reasons for letting go of the dream or transforming it. If you step back from the whirlwind of the emotion, you probably will find that your happiness does not depend on the specific desire you have, in this example, moving. If your emotional and energetic systems do not accept what you know to be factually true, you need to understand why.

Once you set your feet on this new path, grace will likely carry you along. All sorts of things become clear. They were probably already there; you just couldn't see them before. Anything that helps you see the situation with new eyes or generates new questions is useful for inspiration. It might be a conversation with a friend, trying to put yourself in someone else's shoes, or quotations related to your issue. In my case, I found two quotes about dreams that helped me.

Cherish your visions and your dreams, as they are the children of your soul, the blueprints of your ultimate accomplishments. —Napoleon Hill

Dreams are illustrations from the book your soul is writing about you. —Marsha Norman

Both quotes connected dreams with the soul. I didn't believe souls really cared about houses, so I wondered what my soul was seeking. What ultimate accomplishment was at the heart of the matter? Dissatisfaction had been the driver in my story. I'd rather have the book my soul was writing come out of a desire for something inspiring.

One insight that arose from this exploration was that my soul wanted more beauty; that did not have to mean a new house. Another insight was that my greatest passion was the creative process of making a home; that was the real adventure. I could craft a new richer home in the home we already had. I felt like Dorothy in the movie, *The Wizard of Oz*, when she realizes that her heart's desire is in her own backyard.

I moved my life and spirit, but not my home. In the process, my home has become more beautiful, and my family loves it all the more. While I can't see my spirit, I believe it has also become more beautiful. A sense of delight flows through me every day as I walk through my "new" old home who has now become my friend. We fell back in love.

Home Sweet Friend

Your home can be your friend when you work with it
in what Jewish philosopher, Martin Buber, calls an "I–
Thou" relationship rather than an "I–It." In an I-Thou
relationship, you have intrinsic value to me in and of
yourself. Your value isn't in just serving some goal of
mine. It is a stance of respect and dignity. An I–It relationship is one in which I treat something or someone as
having value only as it serves my purposes.

Buber assigned human relationships to the I–Thou
category and things to the I–It category. He saw problems
when we treated humans in an I-It relationship. An example might be the way some organizations treat employees
like expendable merchandise.

Buber would probably call a house a thing. I see a
difference when we apply this insight to homes. To con-
ceive a home in love requires the mutuality of the I–Thou
relationship. Your home becomes a companion. That
relationship will lead you to care for your home in a different way and to want your home to contribute to more
than just your needs. If you treat it as a house, then you
see it as an I–It relationship. The house is there just to
serve you.

If your home is a companion, a new relationship
emerges between your home and you. It may become
your sanctuary, a teacher, and possibly your guide. You
can become its discoverer, beautifier, and caregiver. If you
choose to recognize and engage in this opportunity, something magical and spiritual happens when these roles are
woven together.

Then you begin to ask not only what is your purpose in living, but also, what is your home's purpose in being. Those who are healthiest and happiest usually have defined a purpose that is larger than just their own self-interest. This serves as a reason for living and guides life. So, too, a home with a clear purpose will be happier and make a greater contribution.

A friend walks with us through life. It is someone to be with to laugh, cry, share, inspire, and support us in our dreams. The most important thing they do for us might be to challenge us or invite us on new adventures. People do that, as do our animals. A home can also be your dear friend, as can a piece of land, or a city.

Sam was from Montana and loved the big blue open vistas. Sue was from Maine and loved the glistening blue ocean. They both disliked the cold and moved to San Francisco where they each could have a relationship with the blue vista of the Pacific. They also grew fond of the city. After meeting, they grew fond of each other.

They married and had a child. Owning a house of any type was beyond their means given the high costs of real estate in the city. If they had been willing to move further out of the city, they could have found something. What mattered to them was to be in the city and near the call of the ocean. The larger environment was their home.

They had the same apartment for decades and took care of it as if they owned it, but I never heard the same love in their voices for it as for the city. Their daughter, Jenny, developed similar feelings of attachment. The city was a teacher and land of adventure for her. As a young adult she was considering moving to Maine to try living near her mom's family and developing closer relationships. "But," she commented, "San Francisco will always be home."

Naming Your Friend

There is a long history of naming homes. In villages and small towns, it was natural to give directions to a place by using the resident's name. There usually wasn't any emotion associated with that practice. In larger cities, the development of a postal service was often the impetus for creating an alternative like a numbering system so houses lost their names and became numbers.

In other cases, the name carried meaning to the owner. Thomas Jefferson's home was called Monticello. Winston Churchill named his Cosy Pig. Jane Austen, in *Pride and Prejudice,* refers to Belmont and Pemberly. Other homes took their names from magnificent trees that dominated the lot like Twelve Oaks in *Gone With the Wind* or Orchard House in *Little Women*. Many neighborhoods also bear the name of an early pioneer, allude to the history of the Native American tribe from the region, or relate to geography.

The experience in England is that a name can add value to a house and enhance its competitive position in the market. In the United States, we see a number of these historical devices at work in the naming of developments. Many names imply descriptors about the geography of the land. Many aren't particularly accurate, but they sound great. Some are confusing like Lake Hills. Is it a lake on hills?

Places with emotional connections for the owners are more likely to have a name. Carole Hyder shared her exercise with me about naming your house from her book, *Conversations with Your Home.* You might want to try this idea. I was intrigued because this wasn't about my imposing a name on the house. This was about asking if the house had a name. One night I decided to give it a try. I relaxed, closed my eyes, and let my mind clear. Then, while picturing my home, I thought, "Do you have a name?" I wasn't sure what to expect, but I was open to possibilities.

Almost instantly, the name "Annabelle May" came to me. That surprised me and was fun. It came so fast, and there was a middle name as well as a first name. I don't know any Annabelles. It isn't exactly a common name these days. Where did that come from? I'm intuitive and trust this kind of surprise. At the same time, I am also very logical. I like facts and data and wanted to test this experience.

What's in a name? There is a meaning to names. Like many about-to-be parents, we had consulted books about names when I was pregnant. Names do cycle in popularity throughout different time periods. I decided on a strategy. I listed the characteristics of my home. Then I did some research to test if the descriptors that I listed matched those that went with the names Annabelle and May. Then I used a search engine to find lists of the most popular names during the decade that our house was built.

The characteristics I listed were warm, lovely, graceful, friendly, peaceful, and dependable. I checked several websites. In Hebrew, Annabelle means grace and in Latin, loveable. In Italian, it meant gracefully beautiful. May refers to the month of May and spring. Originally some sources say it was a pet name for Margaret or Mary. Annabelle peaked in popularity in the 1920s. May was still quite popular in the 1920s but peaked in the late 1800s.

I was impressed with the consistency between my intuition and research, so I was content to accept our house was named Annabelle May. I shared it with my family. My daughter, who names everything that matters to her, thought it was a great exercise. Bob just smiled, noncommittally. Subsequently, other pieces came together.

We had some bushes on the south side of the house that had not been doing well for several years. I wandered around the yard looking for inspiration, debating whether to try something new or plant more bushes that were doing well. The healthiest and most prominent bush that seemed like a natural extension sat next to the front steps near our birdbath. I knew it was a hydrangea but couldn't remember the exact kind. I checked the little stick at its roots to find that. It read—Annabelle Hydrangea. That brought a smile and more teasing when I shared the information. It seemed fitting to add more Annabelles to the yard.

Another coincidence occurred as I was writing this story. When I wrote about the name May, something came to mind. Many years ago I had met someone who wrote house histories. I had hired him to write our house history as an anniversary gift for Bob. Checking the house history revealed that the original building permit for our home was taken out on May 2, 1921. The first owner moved in during May of 1922.

Does it matter if a home has a name or if my imagination concocted all this? Having a name for the home does some of the same things that it does for a person. There is a different feeling in thinking of my home as Annabelle instead of the "house" or the address. The name carries our aspirations and reminds us of our values. "It can turn a mere building into an expression of its owner's character; in short, it helps make a house a home," according to Clover Signs, an English organization.

It doesn't matter if you tell the name to anyone else. The meaning is for you and your family. Different members of the household may have different names for the house, just as they do for the children. One parent may call the child by a given name, and the other parent uses a nickname. A name, though, does feel different than a number.

~

Reflections/Suggestions for Another Day:

• What demonstrates to you that your home was conceived in love?

• How would you describe your house versus your home?

• Do you own your house or does it own you?

• How supportive is your home of your most vital dreams?

• How could you work with your house to make it more of a home if it does not meet your needs,?

• If your home is something other than a building, what is it?

• How does your place make you feel at home in the world?

• Do you have an I-Thou or I-It Relationship with your home?

• Listen to the song Hawaii by Israel Kamakawiwo'ole to experience the longing for home.

• Complete the activities suggested in this chapter.

• Invest the time to journal about your experience of house and home.

• Consider naming your home.

Nurtured by Beauty

Interest in beauty manifested early in the development of humankind. Creating colors and applying them to objects carried spiritual and symbolic meaning. From cave drawings to ancient Chinese palaces to pottery making, we find beauty. Somehow it nurtures something important in our souls and hearts.

The Great Pyramid of Giza is the oldest of the Seven Wonders of the Ancient World and the only surviving one. It was built around 2560 BC. Beauty was not limited to the coffins and furnishings for the afterlife of royalty inside the pyramid. The beauty of proportion in building mattered as well. Incredibly, the four sides of the pyramid are almost identical and the sides of the square base are aligned to the four cardinal compass points.

Around 1400 BC, in the Four Corners area of the Southwestern United States, the ancestors of the Pueblo People, the Anasazi, were designing new, more elaborate, and costly forms of pottery. The beauty of these bowls seemed to awaken something rich in the makers. Dozens of new designs were created and the use of bright colors, rather than the traditional black and white, took root. The degree of creativity made it seem as if time had sped up, and pottery manufacturing changed at an unheard of pace.

These decorated bowls also began to appear in distant communities far from their Anasazi makers. Since the bowls made in one place were just as functional as those made in another, the value of the bowls must have been in their beauty. The desire for another's designs, not basic necessity, drove the spread of the bowls. In archaeology, all these indicators are signs of social change and a degree of abundance.

The golden mean, an aesthetically pleasing mathematical concept, especially when applied to art and architecture, has fascinated mankind for over 2400 years. The ancient Greeks studied it and applied it to architecture, including the Parthenon of Athens, which was completed in 438 BC. The temple was dedicated to the goddess Athena and is considered the most important surviving building of Classical Greece. Sculptures and carvings add to its beauty. Its columns were made of marble for the first time and carefully constructed to give the building a sense of grace and proportion.

The Greeks carried their sense of beauty into their homes. These structures were usually made up of two or three rooms that were built around an open-air courtyard. Larger homes might have a kitchen, bath, or private rooms for men and women's activities. The courtyard was the center of life where meals were taken, and storytelling entertained everyone. Women might relax, sew, and talk.

In the Lap of Luxury

Beauty nurtures you in all her forms—majestic mountains, a Leonardo da Vinci painting, or an inviting room—offering delight to your senses and soul. Beauty can heal, inspire, and calm you. There is a certain form of beauty that makes a home. The beauty of all the artwork in a museum causes us to hush our voices and refrain from touching. The beauty we want in our homes encourages conversation and invites us to sink into it or hold it. We don't want to be in awe of it; we want it to be friendly.

Simple beauty is all you need to create a home that refreshes, renews, and inspires you. In the book, *If Aristotle Ran General Motors,* author and philosopher Tom Morris writes, "We all intuitively know that beauty plays a role that can't be duplicated by anything else in its impact on the human spirit, freeing our greatest energies, liberating our deepest insights, and connecting with our highest affections."

Simple beauty has several aspects: it is straightforward and uncomplicated; costs are trouble-free; the feeling of inspiration makes your time and energy investments satisfying and fun. In addition, you or someone you love often is involved in the creation. It is not uncommon for it to be an on-going journey of many small consistent acts leading to harmony. There is flexibility in these descriptors. Your unique situation, talents, and resources will change the interpretation of straightforward, uncomplicated, costly, or inspirational.

Flowers are a lovely example of this beauty. You can

keep a plant or bouquet of flowers straightforward, uncomplicated, and inexpensive. Your participation is minimal: cut the stems, add water and a vase, and refresh the water. Then enjoy.

Some of us need a plant or two in every room. It is as if we need a mini-conservatory of our own. If you cannot keep something alive, then stick to bouquets or acquire a photo or painting. Even calendars with a flower theme can work. Use "flowers" broadly to mean whatever in nature delights you. Maybe it is the tree outside your window or the sun playing on the leaves.

Flowers are clearly important to people across the planet and history. In early times and today, they provided food and medicine to people. Even ancient cave people left flowers in burial sites. The ancient Greeks dedicated flowers to the gods and crowned people with wreaths of blossoms and leaves for the Olympic winners. Turkey developed a concept of flowers as symbols that the Europeans adopted. Books were written about the symbolic meaning of different flowers. In Colonial times, a man could pledge loyalty without ever saying a word by giving a bouquet of violets.

We often send flowers to people in the hospital. At an emotional level, this is a way of saying you care and hope the person heals fast. Research data on the influence of plants suggests that you are also improving the physical recovery rate of those hospitalized.

A recent study at Kansas State University examined the effect of flowers and plants on ninety patients recovering from appendectomies. Patients who had rooms with flowers and plants had "lower blood pressure and heart rates, lower ratings of pain, anxiety, and fatigue, and more positive feelings and higher satisfaction about their rooms when compared with patients in the control group."

In *Beauty and the Soul,* Piero Ferucci looks at the impact of the absence of beauty. He discusses how James Hillman, one of a handful of psychologists, "has emphasized the importance of beauty and the tragedy of its repression." He asks what is the cost of ugliness: "What does it cost in absenteeism, in sexual obsession, school drop-out rates, overeating and short attention spans; in pharmaceutical remedies and the gigantic escapism industries of wasteful shopping, chemical dependency . . . could the causes of major social, political, and economic issues of our time also be found in the repression of beauty?"

If beauty or its absence can have all these effects, surely those plants and flowers that adorn your home create healing as well. The important thing is to look at that beauty daily with intention. The intention could be a reminder of the awe we had as children when we first saw beauty. It could be about love, hope, renewal, and healing. It could even have a global meaning. Perhaps caring for a plant is a way to ground you in the soil or to offer it as a small prayer for the larger planet. The only right answer is the one in your heart and soul.

Tom's backyard is beautiful and full of meaning. Everyone who enters it invariably sinks into one of the chairs on the deck and soaks up the beauty. To you it may look complex, expensive, and a lot of work, but given his gifts, resources, and joy, his creation fits the definition of simple beauty. The yard originally had a small grassy area of flat ground. The rest of it went steeply uphill with some small bushes along a fence at the top.

Years of incremental changes have converted it into something unique and delightful. Now there are several levels of deck where it was flat, a little bridge provides a walk over a recessed garden, and the hillside is covered in shrubs, flowers, and sculptures. Three cats patrol it to their hearts' delight.

Recently, he had a whole new vision of a path that would wind up through the hillside landscaping. Brick-work edges contain the pebbled path. Now he can weed, plant, and water with much more ease. More importantly, people can go for a walk over hill and dale in what is a relatively small area.

Once he had his vision, he said it was a straightforward project. The costs did not strain his budget, especially since he did the work himself. It was a great deal of heavy lifting, but he is a strong guy and loves doing it. His wife, Carole, says the yard is like his child. He can get lost out there for hours, forgetting to eat, rest, or think about anything else. She explains that doing the work himself is meaningful because as he works his imagination takes hold, seeing new opportunities in the flash of a moment.

When we are being fully filled by beauty, love, engagement, work or play, we enter a time warp. It's described in different ways: I lost all sense of time, time stood still, and time flew by. In his book, *Flow: The Psychology of Optimal Experience,* Mihály Csíkszentmihályi explores his theory that people are most happy when they are in a state of *flow*—a state of complete focus and intense joy. Homes offer us many opportunities to experience this.

Being in Tom's garden is even better than visiting a retreat center or high-end resort. You experience a different kind of luxury, one that has nothing to do with lavishness or extravagance. Simple beauty fills us in so many ways. Often when we hear the word luxury, we tend to think of it as requiring money—lots of money—but it doesn't have to be that way. How does a person initiate inspiration and flow?

Earlier I mentioned Wendy, who made her kitchen entrance a little more luxurious with twenty-five dollar curtains. The entrance was filled with jackets and shoes. As her children got older, there was that much more "stuff." She decided it was time to do something about it. We were talking about what she wanted. The obvious answer was a real closet with hangers and shelves, but that would cost money she didn't want to spend. She had put her energy into trying to keep things organized instead, but that wasn't solving her frustration. Even when it was organized, it still seemed messy to her.

I suggested she use the Five Whys, a quality improvement tool. It is a simple tool that helps get to the heart of the matter and suggests alternatives. You just keep asking why about five times. Each "why?" builds on the answer from the previous "why?" This is one way to get to start ideas flowing. Here is how Wendy's experience went.

First, she had to create the right question since she was ruling out a closet. So it became . . .

Q. Why do I want something like a closet by the back door?

A. Because I don't like seeing all the jackets, scarves, hats.

Q. Why don't I like that?

A. Because it detracts from my nice, clean, well-organized kitchen.

Q. Why does it detract?

A. Because it doesn't fit well and is messy.

Q. Why doesn't it fit?

A. Because everything else is a creamy white smooth surface, and then there is a partial wall of stuff.

Q. Why couldn't it be a creamy white surface?

A. I'd like that. Let me think how to do it.

There are usually five "Why" questions before you get to an insight, but it could be fewer or more than five. The point at which you stop asking "why" is when the question intrigues you rather than irritates you, and it shifts your thoughts to possibilities. Then solutions begin to flow. In this case, she stopped and thought, "What could I put there that covers everything, is inexpensive, and creamy white?"

Her answer was to buy a creamy white curtain that had some texture to it. Everything disappeared behind it. The eyesore was gone, yet she still had easy access to everything behind it. The fabric also made the entryway softer and inviting. It was a small luxury solving a big irritant. Before the exercise, her attention was so focused on what she didn't like that she had trouble seeing alternatives that she would like. Once she had the breakthrough, it was simple, inexpensive, and satisfying.

Enhance What You Love

Whether you have just moved or are contemplating improving your dwelling, a good place to start is with enhancing what you love. Something attracted you to this place and kept you here, so work with what is already present.

Most of us do not have the resources to implement everything at once if we get inspired to engage in new acts of beauty. We want to start small, especially because of the elements of time and trouble free costs. If decorating or remodeling costs are going to leave us with worry, stress, and a financial squeeze, then we are violating the elements of trouble-free costs and harmony.

Mia found a duplex to rent after she graduated and started her job. She loved the oak wainscoting, floors and the west facing bay window. She chose paint colors to enhance the woodwork and arranged furniture and area rugs to spotlight the oak floors. She added two Chinese brush paintings above the wainscoting. Mia drew additional attention to the bay window with a striking, large, hanging plant and two large floor plants. She bought a pretty antique plant stand and added a lucky bamboo plant with three stalks for happiness. In Feng Shui, bamboo represents the thriving elements of wood and water in balance.

Judy and her husband, Allen, had bought their first home. It was a story-and-a half house built in the 1950s. One of the things they most liked was the family room that had been an addition by the previous owner. They expected to spend many evenings in that room. The focal point of the room was a large fireplace in the center of the wall opposite the open arch as you entered from the dining room.

The room was a little dark with three small windows shaded by a large silver maple tree in the backyard. The brickwork was quite dark, and the fireplace mantel was narrow. Painting the room a sunny yellow helped lighten it. Judy experimented with painting her bricks. Her new colors altered the whole feeling of the fireplace and made the room more inviting. Allen built a wider mantel to display two special wedding gifts. The renovation was fun, inexpensive, and a collaborative effort in their new home.

Jack and Lois had been married for thirty years. Their kids were grown and had homes of their own. Jack and Lois had the means to build a new home that would meet their future needs. They had traveled a great deal, both for work and pleasure, including living in Europe for five years when Jack was promoted to head a division of his company in France. Art had become a passion during their travels. Every piece had a story that brought back fond memories.

They worked with an architect to design a new home around things they loved. During the design process, they received exciting news; they were about to become grandparents. That brought a new dimension to the design of their home. How could they have a home that was a fun place for a grandchild and safe for their art?

The architect suggested a playroom or even a little suite of rooms for sleepovers. "No," they said, "If we need to segregate anything, it should be the art, not the child." So they worked together to create safe places in various rooms for the objects and added a large art room with lovely double doors that could be closed.

Finally, they had room for the proper display of treasured items. And they had a home for all those they cherished. Subsequently, they wondered if the house would have been less welcoming and comfortable without the changes they made for a child.

When you have been somewhere for a long time, you might have more trouble seeing new opportunities, but they are there. Even a room that you have recently redecorated might perk up even more with that one additional touch. Layer by layer, you can add depth, beauty, and interest.

I've made dozens of changes to my kitchen in our thirty plus years in our home. Most of them made it a more pleasant room, but I wanted two more elements. None of the changes had risen to the level of meaningful. In addition, it did not have that unifying element of green that runs through my home.

I had the itch to do a small project on a rainy Saturday to resolve my two areas of discontent. The soffit above the kitchen work area attracted my attention; it seemed to want something more. The area was about twelve inches high and was painted pearl white on all four sides.

After considering a number of options, none of which had staying power, I took a walk through the rest of the house looking for some kind of stimulus. I found it. It was my special ivy. While we were on our honeymoon,  my mother-in-law cut and rooted slips of ivy from my wedding bouquet. When I discovered that ivy stood for eternal life, friendship, and commitment in marriage, that information compounded the meaningfulness of Mother's action. The ivy flourished for over thirty years adorning various rooms and our relationship over the course of its life.

The thought of capturing the ivy in a new way inspired me. Maybe I could find a stencil of the ivy leaves and paint a strand of it around the whole soffit area. I was excited about that idea. Fortunately, the local craft store had exactly what I wanted. Armed with the stencil, paint, and brushes, I went home to experiment.

I had never stenciled a wall before. Through trial and error, I achieved the desired effect and color. The leaves looked natural, like my plant. The whole project took a day and about $30. It added meaning, color, and a special touch to the kitchen that has stood the test of time. Small details make a difference. Learning something new and being creative were satisfying as well.

Fireplaces, like kitchens and dinner tables, touch

some elemental aspect of yourself; they are the ancient fire around which the tribe bonds. They have a gravitational pull to them. Bob and I were homebound due to a snowstorm one Saturday. We lit a fire in our built-in wood burning stove and curled up with books, but for a change I couldn't stay focused. I was in the mood for something physical and creative.

Our fireplace stared at me; I returned the stare. The previous owners had painted the brick, and we had continued to do the same. It was white, somewhat bland. What was it that I appreciated about the fireplace that called for more attention? It has an unique configuration of brick. Unlike the traditional horizontal row upon row of brick, ours was different. It has both horizontal and vertical rows that form an interesting geometric design; the single color paint made the design subdued and unnoticeable.

I imagined what it would look like if two colors of paint were used to bring attention to the patterns. Using construction paper for samples, I cut and taped them to the bricks trying different approaches. Something interesting was emerging, but it wasn't clear yet which configuration was best. Lovely natural stone installed in the hearth flooring area suggested color possibilities.

It was time to try paint. I brought up every paint can from the basement that had any of the stone tones and painted different colors on various bricks. Choice can be confusing. I was on the right path but wasn't sure which branch to follow. When in doubt, let it settle in, is my motto.

Insight came later. It sneaked up one night and said, "Paint the grout, not the bricks." I repainted the bricks cream again, and then applied the green sage from the walls to the grout. I also painted the bricks across the top and down one row n each side creating a frame of green (see book cover). I hit the jackpot. It added just the right amount of color so that it didn't look like another sage green wall. It brought out the pattern, and it added a depth that was quite satisfying. The fireplace had a new elegance, and the room came together in a new unity.

Color My World Pleasing

Color fashion surrounds us; it can nurture or dominate you. Color is Big Business. From clothing to paint to furnishings to skin products, there is someone always trying to tell you what you *should* like.

Color influences. Schools and hospitals, as well as malls, are more aware of the impact of color. Teachers report changes in children's behavior after classrooms are painted a more calming color. Symbolic meaning is another reason color matters. It is somewhat culturally dependent. In the United States, white is associated with innocence and weddings; in the East, it is the color of mourning and funerals.

Different countries or regions will have different color pallets due to weather, nature, and tradition. People in Sweden paint their homes red, blue, yellow, and other bright happy colors to brighten their long winters. Even the bridges and highways in the Santa Fe, New Mexico area are painted, adding interest and connecting with symbols to their rich Native American heritage. When we were in Greece we saw many buildings whitewashed that reflected sunlight with blue roofs that matched the seas.

So color in your home has an effect, not just on how lovely it looks, but also on health and the emotional environment. It can contribute to or undermine harmony and warmth. The blend of colors of food on our plate enhances or reduces our appetite. Knowing what works for you may require doing some research on the impact of colors or gathering your own experiential data. Pay attention, and take note of how you feel mentally and emotionally when you are around different colors.

Connie and Bill's six-year-old son, Ben, began having trouble sleeping at night. He couldn't settle down, and if he woke up during the night, he ended up in his parent's bed; it was the only way to get him back to sleep. In the morning it was hard to wake him up in time to get to school. This was all new behavior.

A visit to their pediatrician did not find any physical issues, but the doctor suggested that they think about whether there had been any changes at home or school in the preceding weeks. Connie could think of one big change. They had redecorated Ben's room. He had been delighted with his new fire-engine theme room and its bright reds and yellows. Connie was disheartened. What was she supposed to do—remake the room again? Bill suggested she call a cousin who was a nurse and had three children. Maybe she would have a simpler idea.

Connie called Marilyn and explained the situation. They arranged for Marilyn and her kids to come for a visit. When Connie lamented her decorating, Marilyn reassured her and offered a few suggestions. "It's a great playroom," she said, "and you were paying attention to what Ben loves. The problem isn't the whole room. Ben just needs a quieter spot by his bed. Maybe if you replace the sheets (which also had fire engines on them) with a more soothing blue, take the red spread off at night, and add some curtains to cover the lower bunk bed area, then he would have a quieter little cave for sleeping. Hopefully, that will solve the issue." Connie tried all the changes, and within a short period of time Ben was sleeping again.

Color is personal. There is room for trends, advice from paint store experts, or interior designers. What is critical to remember is that your intentions, and the people you love should be the drivers of any decision. Everything else is just data. What you, your family, and your home need may be different from the current trends. When it comes to your home, you should be able to live in the luxurious lap of the colors that delight your soul, rather than have to follow the crowd. If it is an outside color, it is respectful to consider the impact on the people who will have to look at it all the time.

I do not have the same eye for color that some friends do. In particular, I do not have the same eye for color that an interior designer has. Alecia, our interior designer, and I met at my daughter's school. Our children were friends and in the same class. Bob and I had redone our living room and dining room several times over the years in different colors. We had liked them, but we never were as satisfied as we'd anticipated.

After Bob and I decided to stay in our home and give it new life, the living room rose to the top of the list for attention. Our exquisite oriental rug would be the inspiration for the room. Alecia and I had discussed how we used the room and what we wanted to change. We agreed a new wall color would bring out the warmth and richness in the rug.

Alecia taught me the wisdom of buying a quart of paint and applying it in a generous sized area on two or more walls. Then she said to live with it for a day or two under different light conditions, be attentive to how it changed in color, and how it affected the whole room. Often, we would try more than one color, even just slightly different shades of the same color. The effect was informative and sometimes startling.

I resisted that at first, not realizing what a difference it could make, and because it seemed wasteful. My strategy was penny-wise and pound-foolish. Her approach cost a little more in the short run, but since we were going to live with that color for many years, it was a wise long-term investment. Ask your local paint store how to donate the unused paint if, like me, that is a concern of yours.

The color she recommended we try was a sage green that I hadn't even noticed was in the rug; it wasn't one of the dominant colors. Its potential was obvious the minute we painted a section of the wall. Over the next few days, I was amazed how different it looked in sunlight as well as in the light cast by lamps in the dark of night. It was perfect.

My family also liked the color. Four people have asked if they could copy me. Each had chosen it for a different room—a living room, a bedroom, an office, and a music room. Many guests may not have copied it, but have commented on how comfortable and welcoming it is. We extended it to the dining room and the upper stairway.

That experience was thoughtprovoking. You can enhance visual harmony by having one color flow through the whole place. If you have a room and color that is at the heart of the home you could extend it to adjoining spaces. If the color is a powerful one for you, you might discover there are already subtle elements of it in other rooms found in photographs, pillows, or living plants.

You can still have distinct rooms with interesting and satisfying colors but create this weaving together at the same time. Separate and united. Distinct and connected. A living system and a patchwork quilt. That can be a wonderful metaphor for your family. You can be individuals and a whole. You can have different tastes, but they can work harmoniously. Home nurtures us and models important aspects of relationships in surprising ways.

Shannon and Tim were challenged by the color that their nine-year-old son, Sam, wanted in his bedroom. He wanted midnight blue with stars and planets so that he could have a Star Wars theme. His parents felt the room would be too dark, hard to paint over after this passing phase, and the color did not go with the rest of their home's colors. Imagination and collaboration came to the rescue. They painted one wall the color he wanted, and the other three walls were a complementary sand color that did coordinate with the rest of the house and solved their other reservations. They suggested to Sam that the second color represented Tatooine, a Jedi desert planet. Then he was good to go with the change.

Integrate Diversity

You can love something too much. You can also follow a good rule of thumb too far. Kevin finished college and rented his first apartment in an older building. Since he was partial to green and gold, he didn't mind the older harvest gold appliances and light brown carpet. He was excited to have his own bachelor pad and was determined to do it his own way. He made one concession to his mother; she could make curtains, but he would specify the colors.

He knew that things should match. After living in an apartment with four other males during college where everything was mismatched and clashed, he wanted his place to be a big step-up. He bought a green and gold plaid matching recliner and sofa. His new lamp was green marble with a white shade that had a gold rim. The small table with two chairs fit in the small alcove to the kitchen; the chairs had green cushions. The framed picture over the sofa was of a field of golden reeds and a pond with geese flying over. His mother was a bit overwhelmed when she arrived with his green curtains.

I love wood, especially oak. The number one thing that attracted me to our house was the amount of oak. We also had an oak dining room set as well as other oak furniture. As Alecia and I were continuing to work on the living room, one day we were discussing a new coffee table. I was thinking a mission style one. Alecia looked at me and said, "Do you like *anything* that isn't wood?"

That started an interesting conversation with a number of helpful takeaways. One was that beauty is enhanced by diversity and balance. Alecia pointed out I needed a blend of the basic elements and not just one. This was ancient knowledge. Many traditions talked about earth, air, fire, and water. In Feng Shui, they refer to wood, fire, earth, metal, and water.

Conceptually, I understood her point but resisted. I knew wood; it was familiar and comfortable. I knew the grains, the effect of different colors of stains, and how to care for it. It stood the test of time. Every house I had lived in had beautiful wood. I associated it with warmth. Other materials seemed cold to me with the exception of earth, which for me meant plants.

I had unconsciously slipped into an over reliance on what was familiar and part of my roots. It wasn't that I didn't like other things or that they weren't also beautiful, but they were foreign. It was time to expand. Alecia encouraged me to explore new terrains. "Go and browse. Focus on any coffee table that isn't wood. Notice how it feels and looks, as well as what you like and don't like. Then, if it is near some wood furniture, notice how they affect each other as companions."

I found a stone table that fascinated me once I really paid attention to it. It was rectangular instead of my normal oval. It had six 1' x 1' stone slabs with different colors running through it. I had forgotten that stone had grains as well as wood. The colors were muted and would complement my living room's oriental rug and paint color. In addition, they made the vibrancy of the rug colors stand out.

You might have fun and get inspired with a new idea if you pay a visit to your rooms as if you were new to the home. Using the Five Elements is a nice lens through which you may see a new land. Water could be represented by the color black, or in a water fountain, watering can, vase of flowers, faucet, or a water bowl for the cat or dog. Earth could appear in your room by the colors yellow or brown, or by the use of clay, rocks, bricks, or ceramics. The color red, a fireplace, or a candle could imply Fire. Metal is evident by the color white, metal furniture or metal sculptural pieces. Wood is evident by the color green, plants, flowers, or vertical lines.

The Elements originated out of the lives of an agrarian society. Water nourished the plants (Wood), Wood stoked up Fire, Fire left its ashes to enrich the soil (Earth), Earth produced Metals, and Metal created condensation (Water), which begins the cycle all over. This is known as the Constructive Cycle of the Elements.

Are You Balanced?

• Take a pad of paper and form a chart on it with the names of your rooms down the left hand side and the Five Elements along the top.

• Tour your rooms making check marks or notes about which elements are present in which rooms.

• Notice your results, then look for the lack of an element or an overdose of it.

• Give thought to the meaning of any pattern that you see such as the total absence of some element or an overabundance of anything.

• Explore if there is a new touch of some element that would add a pleasant or meaningful touch to that room or if you need to reduce an element.

• Move things from room to room to achieve balance.

Using the Five Elements in creating your home could be a source of nourishment. So far, I have been referring to them as objects in a home. You could also look at them as to how they contribute to relationships. What earth-like element in your home nurtures the potential of all the occupants? It could be inside or outside. Antonio grew up in a farming area. His family and other workers gathered around a big tree every day to eat lunch and talk. He says that tree was an important part of home. It heard every-one's dreams including his parents' wish that he and his brother would go to college when they grew up. He loved that tree, and it held his aspirations.

How does your home "water" each person's gifts as well as the relationships? When fire erupts—disagree-ments of all types—how is the burn controlled so that it ends up generating warmth and productive "ash?" What metal—mental—tools help cut through all the ideas, desires, and doubts that have taken root in the home so that the harvest is plentiful? How are existing and new plants—ideas, desires, and doubts—explored?

Uncover Beauty

Occasionally you know there is hidden beauty to be found in your dwelling place; it might be inside or out-side. Other times, your place has some clues that it takes time to discover. Time and thoughtfulness will unearth it, and you will be glad you did.

Phil and Greg bought an old historic mansion that had fallen on hard times. They planned to use part of it as liv-ing space and part of it as an event center. They knew there was obvious beauty that just needed some loving care. They also suspected there were secrets to be revealed.

There was a large foyer with a nondescript chandelier mounted from the average plaster ceiling. Replacing the chandelier was an obvious starting point, but as they thought about it, the ceiling seemed out of place for the age of the mansion. Investigation revealed a stunning hand-painted tile ceiling hidden above the false ceiling. Another large room had been converted into a modern looking office area. The fireplace was enclosed in a wood surround that was incompatible with the house and the fireplaces in the other rooms. Removal revealed lovely stonework.

Malik and Aaliyah were proud of their new small home. The original interior windows were in decent shape, but the outside windows were aluminum combinations. The first winter convinced them that something needed to be done. The combinations were flimsy, rattled, and had not blocked the cold. They had no experience with weatherization; however, their neighbor, Josh, had lots of experience.

They talked about caulking or putting up plastic coverings in the fall. Aaliyah thought that would look ugly, and the sun would not come through. Then Josh mentioned that whoever had replaced the windows might not have bothered to get rid of the original wood storm windows. They unearthed them in the garage rafters and found screens in the attic under tarps. With a little advice from Josh and Malik's carpentry skills, they removed the aluminum windows and reinstalled the wood windows. First, though, Aaliyah sanded and painted the frames a color that added more interest and beauty to the exterior. Their gas bill also began better looking; that was a great bonus.

We knew our old house well. After thirty years, it still had secret surprises. The aluminum soffits, gutters, and window trim were deteriorating. If you touched them, you or your clothes ended up white. Hail had also had an impact. Our interior windows were ninety-years-old and in need of attention. The removal of the exterior aluminum combination windows and trim would have to be coordinated with the replacement of the interior windows.

We were concerned. With twenty-eight double hung windows, a piano window, two fireplace windows, plus five basement windows, replacement was going to be costly. We also wondered what was hiding under the aluminum soffits. Did a previous owner cover them up because of rot, or was it just for easier maintenance? If the wood had rotted, that would add to our costs. We were walking around the house during the late winter contemplating our changes. Looking up at the snow-laden roof, we discussed the white aluminum boxy squares that were at the peaks of the house and intermittently under the soffit. They seemed peculiar, and we wondered what was underneath.

In the spring, the contractor started removing the aluminum soffits, shutters, and the squares. The most gorgeous corbels (A corbel is a piece of wood or cement that juts out from the wall that might be decorative or load bearing) appeared. More accurately, they had the potential to be gorgeous once they were sanded, and painted. Suddenly, we had nineteen total great new design

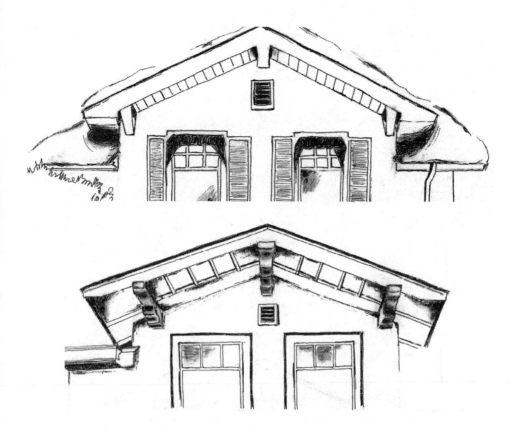

elements around the whole house to work with and paint
as part of the detailing of the exterior. They were curved
with many details so distinct from the aluminum box
shapes. We painted them the same rust color as the trim
on the windows, which added interest against the peanut
colored wood frames. Once they were restored, our home
seemed to lift her head with more confidence and pride.
She was whole again.

   We discovered a second hidden beauty. We had always
thought it was a little odd that the kitchen floor was
noticeably higher than the adjoining dining and living

room floors. The threshold separating the rooms was close to three-fourths of an inch higher than the floor. Skip is my "house doctor." He is a carpenter and builder who can do almost anything. He was doing some work for me one day so I asked him about the floor heights.

His best guess was that there were many layers of flooring on top of each other. Maybe the original floor was still there and would likely be maple. He suggested moving a small cabinet on the side of the stove and cutting out a good size patch if I wanted to know the full story. He had to go through seven layers of tile, linoleum, plywood, and then more tile and linoleum. Finally, we could see the original floor.

There it was—maple—just waiting for us to find it. Excitement was followed by concern. What if we tore all those layers up and the floor was in bad condition? Skip said the flooring above the basement steps would have been a high traffic area, so if the floor was good there, the odds were that the whole kitchen might be redeemable. If it wasn't in good shape, we could deal with just that area without having to redo the whole kitchen.

The test area proved to be in good shape as well; it just needed refinishing. Then it was time to remove the whole floor except for under the cabinets. We didn't want the cost of moving all of them out to take up the floor. We knew some day they would have to be replaced anyway. Skip created new molding that was wider than the old molding and hid the difference between the floor levels under the cabinets and the refinished maple floor. Curiosity, discovery, work, and creative problem solving had put beauty back on display.

Warm Furry Beauty

Pets are beauty in action and often are barometers of the
harmony or disharmony of your home. Come home sad or
angry, and they will know and respond. If laughter heals,
then we should pay pets a high salary. You can watch the
most hysterical antics in your own living room. Even if you
don't have a pet, you can enjoy a laugh on TV or You-
Tube, if you watch the antics of other people's pets.

Terry has a beautiful Ragdoll cat named Chloe. She
is a semi-longhaired cat with captivating blue eyes. Her
body is white, and she has brown markings on her face,
legs, tail, and ears. The Ragdoll cat is bred to produce
affectionate animals more interested in people and more
calm with children than many other cats. She has a
perch attached to one of the family room windows. She
stretches luxuriously on her honey velvet cushion as she
looks at her family. "Don't you want to stroke my soft
glorious fur?" she seems to ask.

Mookie is a longhaired tortoise shell cat with an
attitude. Her shiny black coat has orange, white and tan
running through it. Add an orange nose, and you can
understand why she was originally referred to a Spookie,
a witch's cat. Mookie allows Francine and Dan to live
with her. She started life as a stray kitten that made her
way into the good life twelve years ago.

Mookie blesses different parts of the house with her
beauty as she follows her daily circuit. She begins the day
at station #1 while sunning in the east facing kitchen bay
window and resting on a pretty hand-made felted pad.
In a little while she gives a few head bumps to the most
available ankles announcing she is ready for action. After

the morning chores of being brushed, petted, and fed, she moves to station #2 on her daily route. She has a favorite chair, also padded, in the basement where it is quieter and cooler for her morning nap. By early afternoon, it is time to grace station #3—either the porch or the bed, depending on the weather.

Dinner is to be served promptly along with more attention. She does not approve of the new requirement that she work for her dinner in order to get some exercise. Her toy will only provide her with food if she rolls it around. Mookie, you see, does not care that she has lost her girlish shape. When bedtime rolls around, she fusses at Francine and Dan if they are not punctual.

During all the in-between times of the day, she has worked hard and earned her keep by her endearing purrs, swishing tail, and other displays of affection.

Sheila has loved dogs her entire life; a house without a dog could never be home. Her two Keeshonds were good looking, and their coats shone. Once her daughter was grown, she still had more love to give beyond her own two dogs and cat. She decided to try starting a part-time doggie day care in her home. She took her basement, which was already set up as the dog center, and made it even more functional and enticing for visiting dogs.

It was painted a bright cheery color. There was a two-tiered grooming table by the sink. A rolling cabinet with drawers housed everything that a pup could need. Shelves contained fluffy towels and clean sheets for the kennels and big bins of treats, some homemade. Each of her dogs had his or her own permanent kennel. There were two to spare for visiting dogs. Toys and training equipment finished the décor.

Eventually, she and her husband moved out of the city and built a home on several acres, which gave her even more room for her passion. The new kennels were even nicer than the last, and now she could have a dog door connecting to a ramp that led to the outdoor play area. That area had both a sunny open area for romping and a shaded spot for resting. Winding trails through the two acres and around the pond in the back were fun for the two-legged and four-legged members of the family. Wildflowers, colorful birds, and an occasional deer accompanied them.

Maybe a house does try to attract its owners. Sheila's property appeals to nature and animal lovers. If houses have a way of enticing the owner they seek, then so do pets. The matchmaking that happens with our pets is fascinating. We may have our practical requirements we want met about size or breed, but in the end the choice rests on something intangible.

When I moved to Minneapolis after graduate school, I found an apartment not far from Bob. I furnished it sparsely. The apartment was a way station, a place to eat, sleep, and store my stuff. I had cobbled together hand-me-down furniture. There wasn't much life in that place.

There was a small family-run pet store nearby. One night, Bob and I went for a walk and found the store was open. We were looking, not buying, although I really wanted a dog. There were four dogs and a few cats. I fell in love with a cute little pup that had black wavy fur with white around her muzzle and down her neck. She was a mix of Toy English Spaniel and Pomeranian.

Her eyes caught me; they seemed wise. She was lying quietly looking as if she were sizing me up while the other puppies were yipping and pawing at their kennels. She was operating on the principle of attraction. When I moved closer and put my hand out, she raised her head and assessed the situation. She decided to engage. She scooted forward a little and gently licked my finger. I melted on the spot. I named her Athena, after the Greek goddess of wisdom.

After I brought her home, that old frayed apartment acquired a new warmth, energy, and sparkle for the rest of my time there. She was smart. No matter how I tried to confine her within the kitchen, she found a way out. She would be there at the door to greet me every night. While she waited, she had one bad habit—she tugged at the worn carpet. As she grew from a few pounds to twelve pounds her ability to rip carpet increased. I suppose it was a game to her and initially helped with teething. By the time I left the apartment, I was sure I was leaving my security deposit behind, but I would never have given her up.

An animal isn't right for everyone; they can complicate your life. For many of us, though, adding these companions to our homes, enriches our lives. Approximately 62% of U.S. homes have a pet. There are 75 million dogs and 88 million cats spread among them. In a recent survey, Americans were asked what they would donate to if given $100,000. Animal welfare was the fourth most frequent choice.

Why do we have such a love affair with pets? Unlike farm animals, they do not produce goods to sell or do work to earn their keep. According to the Center for Disease Control, there are numerous health benefits to having a pet such as having a positive effect on blood pressure, cholesterol and triglyceride levels, and reducing feelings of loneliness. It seems fitting that color, nature, and pets all have similar impacts on the well-being of humans. They all share the attributes of beauty.

The bond between pets and their owners has been measured in intriguing ways. In *Dogs That Know When Their Owners Are Coming Home,* scientist Rupert Sheldrake discusses research on dogs and other animals that seem to have precognition about their owners. Using video equipment and monitors, he has tracked the behavior of pets who seem particularly connected to their owners and know when their owners have left work, boarded a plane, or even just thought about going home. They have altered time and situations to test whether the pet is responding to habit or something else. The results are amazing. He raises some very intriguing questions. Here are my versions of his questions:

• How might animals make people more human and make home, more homelike?

• What if our pets have intentions that they communicate to us?

• Do domesticated animals have intelligences and emotions that are different from animals in the wild? That is, how might having a home change their intelligence and emotional quotient?

• What might our pets teach us about home, life, and ourselves?

Underneath it all, my best guess is that for many of us, pets touch something deep in our being that evokes being loved and wanting to give love. There is a bond so deep that even when we feel annoyed or angry, we still forgive and love them as we try to repair or replace the spoiled rug or gnawed chair. Our pets make us laugh. We feel loved and welcomed home. They nurture us with a beauty all their own.

∼

Reflections/Suggestions for Another Day:
• What could you do to make your home feel more luxurious?
• What are three meaningful things that attracted you to your home?
• How could you enhance those three things?
• How do the colors of your rooms affect you and your family?
• What colors, things, or feelings unite your home?
• What could you do to enhance your ability to see your home with new eyes?
• Where might there be hidden beauty in your home?
• How balanced from the perspective of the Five Elements is your home?
• How does your home provide for the Five Elements in relationships?

• If you have or want to have pets, how do they contribute to the beauty of your home?

• Try the Five Whys exercise to gain new insights on an issue facing you.

Awakened by Creativity

We love the "aha" moment. In that moment a discovery registers in our consciousness. It doesn't matter what the discovery is. We experience delight and satisfaction; a path appears where there was only forest. We wake up ready to go. There are misconceptions about creativity. One is that it is reserved for the gifted, the artist, or the composer. Humans are born creative until someone stills their song or some forms of education drive it into hiding.

Another misconception is that creativity is associated with big impressive projects—a new scientific discovery, going to the moon, or building an art center. Those are great feats, but where would we be without a needle and thread, the leash for the dog, the dyes that create color in paints and clothing, or even a garage. Who invents these things? Who concerns themselves with making them appealing to the eye?

The word garage originated from a French verb "garer." The meaning was to shelter or protect merchandise. As cars became a more common element of society, the need arose for a new type of outbuilding. The idea of a barn or a carriage house was already common as a place that protected the horses and buggy. So it was not surprising that this new mode of transportation would be linked to the old idea of storage. At first, some people co-lodged the car with the horses and buggy, but the smell of manure found its way into the car and doomed that idea. Public garages were tried, but as the number of cars grew, people wanted their vehicles close to home.

The first buildings on owner's property were simple sheds. The most challenging part was the door. A large door was needed for letting the car in and out, so barn doors were converted into garage doors. It was a double door, attached with strap hinges requiring that the door open outward. Unfortunately, the hardware of the hinges couldn't handle the amount of use and were troublesome. In addition, there was dissatisfaction over having to shovel every time it snowed so that the doors could open outward.

The first innovation was to create a sliding track for the doors, so they could be moved sideways within the garage, and not have to open outwards. That required a garage to have double the width of the door. This led to the cutting of door sections that could fold around corners. Then in 1921, C.G. Johnson invented the overhead door that became the choice of consumers. Five years later he invented the electric garage door opener.

As time passed, garage doors became more than utilitarian. As lots became smaller, the garage had to be placed closer to the home. Architects began to design them to fit with the design of the house. Colonial, French, Mediterranean, Craftsman, and other style doors evolved. Now garages seem to be moving to the front of the houses. The typical double garage door is now said to constitute about 40% of the front of most suburban homes.

Play Time

Adults need playtime almost as much as children. If you think of what playtime does for a child, you can see why it should be a lifetime pursuit. Play is so important, it has been recognized by the United Nations High Commission for Human Rights as a right of every child. That is major league stuff.

Anthropologist Ashley Montagu believes that one of the reasons that the human species has continued to evolve and been so creative in adapting to different climates, changes in society, and demonstrated the ability to invent is because humans have long childhoods compared to other species. Those childlike traits of curiosity, spontaneity, a sense of wonder, the capacity to play, and experiment all contribute to future adaptability and creative problem solving.

Check the website of the American Academy of Pediatrics. There is a wonderful report, "The Importance of Play in Promoting the Healthy Development of Children and Maintaining Strong Parent-Child Bonds." It discusses the benefits of play covering the broad territories of creativity, decision-making, confidence building, conflict resolution, healthy brains, negotiation skills, leadership, strength building, and weight control. They also discuss socio-emotional development which in organizational speak is called emotional quotient (intelligence) or EQ. You lose some of these benefits if the playtime is too structured and controlled. In the case of children, that means adult control. In the case of adults, it means other adults are too controlling. Companies are spending millions of dollars in training programs for their employees to learn these same things when instead maybe they should encourage more play.

Often we seem to equate play for adults, children, and families as going somewhere and spending money. These are fun things to do and can also be educational and opportunities for personal growth. Our homes are able and willing to also provide these opportunities. It's part of what makes it home—that it can nurture us in these ways.

The choices are endless when we release our imagination. How the single adult as a solo or with friends versus a family will implement play is different, but the definition is the same. Fun, amusing, imaginative, enjoyable, and freeing—all describe play. It is a ritual, like eating, that is necessary to the human spirit. It can include board games, activities like tag, or arts and crafts like knitting and scrapbooking. Fun conversations can include storytelling, word games, or the car game we played as kids guessing words with a few clues. You could have a family book club night. With new technology we can play sports together on Wii Sports or exercise together with Wii Fit and other programs.

Your residence can be a playmate. You can shift tasks
that you don't see as play. Just switch to a different lens.
Cooking, painting a room, quilting, or raking leaves can
be turned into play, if seen through new eyes. A shift
in perspective can even be transformational. Shift hide
and seek into an adult game, and play out the detective
role. Your clues will emerge in the form of questions.
The difference in height between my kitchen and dining
room was what led me to ask, "I wonder why that floor
is higher?" That led to the discovery of the maple floor in
the kitchen.

Play Detective

• Wander through your home looking for hidden
beauty clues, in the form of questions.

• Look for anything that elicits a question from you
such as "I wonder why that is . . . ?"

• Keep a list of these questions as you move from room
to room.

• Repeat this process looking for questions such as
"What if I . . . ?"

• Record those ideas as well.

• Review these lists to see if there is an idea that you
want to pursue.

We've enjoyed visits to Santa Fe and the Georgia O'Keeffe
Museum. On one trip, I noticed that Bob seemed interested in some of her southwest landscape prints, so I
encouraged him to pick his favorites. We framed them
when we returned home and decided that we liked them

in our bedroom. They had a cinnamon color that added a different vitality to our room.

Once they were up, we played with a question, "What if we added more of that color to the room?" We agreed that might be a good idea. Bob informed me that he didn't like our curtains that much. I was willing to retire them. They had provided good service in two different rooms for quite a few years. I found some other sheers that were called "cinnamon spice" as well as three coordinating pillows.

We were very happy with our old room but love this one even more. It changed the room significantly; it felt new. The primary color in the rugs was blue, but the border incorporated other colors. When the curtains went up, the cinnamon in the border appeared. Before, it hadn't seemed to exist. Somehow adding "spice" to the room also seemed like a playful metaphor.

I was repainting the upstairs hallway for probably the fourth time. I had been stuck for years with the idea that the hall needed to be a very light color to add brightness. I had finally eliminated that broken record from my brain and was pleased with the luminescent gray I was now painting.

The woodwork and the linen closet doors and drawers were all antique white. I had intended to just give them a refresher coat. Still, I was so pleased with the walls that I wanted to play some more, be creative, so I reviewed the linen closet with new eyes looking for a hidden opportunity. The drawers had a smooth flat surface, but the doors had panels in them laid out two by two. I had seen them as one unit, but now I saw them as separate elements. I wondered what would happen if I painted the panel the gray color and the rest of the doors the white. When I did it, I discovered it added interest and variety.

New handles for the doors and drawers for the linen closet added to the effect. What had been functional had become beautiful. The final touches for the whole hall were enlargements of some photos from trips to some of nature's wonders like the Grand Canyon, Yosemite, and wildflower fields. We used antique frames that we had in the attic. A hall that was serviceable became engaging.

Creativity is part of the essence of being human—for all of us, not just artists or inventors. It enters every domain of daily life—better meals, good relationships, parenting, a gorgeous wardrobe without a hundred articles of clothing, and a happy life. The very act of problem solving and thinking creatively fills us up in wonderful ways. It feels like a fountain bubbling up and overflowing inside of your being because it puts you in touch with your spiritual essence.

It takes you beyond religion to a personal connection with the Creative force of life. According to artist Michele Shea, "Creativity is . . . seeing something that doesn't exist already. You need to find out how you can bring it into being, and that way be a playmate with God." These adventures help us use a whole part of our brain, soul, and being that are even more important than our intellect and skills. That is one of the gifts our homes give us—a playing field and practicum for beauty and creativity.

Restrictions as an Art Form

Your home may provide you with your most significant opportunity to awaken your creativity. It is a large landscape on which to paint your dreams relating to beauty, meaning, relationships, and purpose. Restrictions of size, budget, time, or any other kind, can be seen as an opportunity. As my friend Magaly once said, "Creativity is not being able to use every color in the spectrum. It's about having only two and making miracles with them."

Switching to that mindset might take some effort, but it is well worth it. A significant life lesson comes with this practice. Feeling restricted to the point that it blocks your creativity is similar to assuming a victim stance, which is counterproductive to creating a meaningful home. You can always do something to add beauty, warmth, or love. Often focusing on what you have can provide a breakthrough. When you already possess something, you start from a place of "having," a place of abundance.

My first experience of trying to stretch a small budget to cover a large room was in college. My roommate and I had left the dorms and rented an apartment. I had my own bedroom. It had one large blank wall and another with a narrow window that provided a view of a dirty brick building across the alley. The third wall consisted of a large built-in closet and the last had the hall door and a radiator. A mattress, box spring, stereo with speakers, and a bookcase finished off the accoutrements for the room. My budget was meager.

Paint was the first step in my effort to claim this room and make it inviting. The purchase of two large colorful pieces of fabric to serve as a spread and curtain was the next step. The skinny single window with no view needed a facelift. Since the fabric was wide enough to cover two windows, I decided to create the illusion that there were two windows. I centered a large rod over the window and let the fabric drape the full width of the rod.

By now, my budget had just under $10 left, and the large blank wall stared at me. Even posters were beyond my budget. The wall needed something about 9' x 7'. Rummaging through what I already owned that might be usable wasn't encouraging. I had two small posters and a skein of yarn. I liked the posters, especially the image of a three mast sailing ship; it symbolized the sense of setting sail in my life. Too bad it was so small.

What could I do with a skein of yarn? An idea hit me. I bought a box of small nails. Very lightly I penciled the major lines of the sailing ship from the poster onto the wall. Once I had the dimensions right, I tapped in the nails at all the major junctures. After trial and error, I wove the yarn around the nails like connecting the dots. My ship covered the wall, and I set sail with $8 still in my pocket.

Another good place to start when you are feeling like you can't have what you want is to find something someone else doesn't want and be open to alternatives. BJ grew up on a farm where the window over the kitchen sink looked out on woods and a river. She loved to wash dishes because she could get lost in the view while her hands were busy. Since she currently lives in a townhouse with no opening to the outer world from her kitchen, she wished for a window with a view.

One day while visiting friends, she had an idea. Her friends were in the midst of remodeling projects in their lovely, older home. At the moment replacing basement windows was in process. BJ noticed the soon-to-be-discarded, weathered, white windows leaning against the basement wall. She loved old window frames anyway, but this one seemed to be just the right size for the space above her kitchen sink.

One of her favorite travel spots is California, and she had postcards from her various favorite places in frames all over the house or tucked in books or drawers. Could she have a postcard scene painted or enlarged and put behind that window frame? Then it could hang over her townhome sink. She could bring California to Minnesota and look out on LaJolla Cove.

Conveniently, her friend, Annie, is an artist who was taking watercolor lessons at the time. BJ shared her idea, and Annie agreed to take a look at the postcard and consider the notion. BJ's postcard began an involved project for Annie because she used it for her art class. She is a perfectionist, so this project became not only a work of art, but also a labor of love—complete with her art instructor's guidance.

BJ was excited thinking that she would have her favorite place captured on paper by a favorite person, behind an old window frame that reminded her of her childhood home. Everything was going to be PERFECT . . . until a slight problem arose. The window frame, according to Annie's art instructor, was much too heavy for the delicacy of the watercolor and could not be used. It would do an injustice to the artwork.

For BJ, this whole project came about because of the

window and the memory it invoked, so getting rid of
the window was a significant issue. Her friends came to
the rescue. They suggested that her dad, who is a good
handyman, make a lighter frame that looked like the window. More trials and tribulations were overcome with the
help of her dad and mom.

Today, a 13" x 33" watercolor of LaJolla Cove, California, hangs above BJ's kitchen sink. It's frame of simple
white wood matches the cupboards that surround the
artwork. For some, that is all they see. As BJ does dishes,
she sees out her "window" to California, as well as into
her heart's memories of her friends, her mom and dad,
and her childhood farm.

Roger thrives on restrictions. It makes everything more
fun as he sees it. Woodworking is in his blood. His grand-
father did it. His dad wanted to but never got the chance.
Roger has made a passion of it. He says, "I can get totally
focused, lost in time. I love every detail, so I do it even when
I'm not at work. Fun and work are one thing for me."

He continued, "I love making something out of nothing. Give me tools, scrap lumber, angle irons and pipes,
and I could make something good that looks like it
belongs. It just comes easy to me. I could take a house
that no one wanted and make it something that a lot of
people would want." When the time came to buy a home,
his wife, Teresa, agreed to a house that she didn't like
because of Roger's skills. She knew two things—Roger
could and would make it a beautiful home, and she has
creative talents as well. Together, the house would get a
new lease on life. And, it did.

Not all of us have this talent or skill, but we all do have imagination, friends, neighbors, and other resources. Tapping into those can add meaning to your projects. Strangers can be a resource, as well, through garage sales. Need to clean out the basement and don't want to pay for things to be hauled away? Want to feel good about giving something that is still useful to someone else, rather than see it go to a landfill? In my area we have a website called Twin Cities Free Market. If you live in the area, you can list things you no longer want and are willing to give away for free and can search for free things you do want. See if your city offers something like this.

My garage gave me a chance to be creative. Since one side of it makes up a large percentage of the view looking from the back of the house into the yard, it was quite prominent and boring. We dressed it up to look like a cottage. First, we added shutters to the window and a flower box hanging from the sill and painted them to match the house colors. Then, we put up trellises and grew vines on both sides of the window. The final touch was a garden flag that hangs in the window. We change it each season from loons for spring to a snow-scape with a cardinal for winter, and a butterfly with fall colors for autumn.

Our garage door became another opportunity to be creative. Most garage doors are quite similar. The major differences are whether they have windows or not, what color they are, and to what degree they are maintained. About 15 years ago, the wear and tear of weather were showing, and the door required a major sanding and painting. I was debating what I saw as my limited choices—white, off white, snow white, cream, beige. They all sounded boring.

Most of the neighbors' garages face the alley. Ours, however, faces the sidewalk that runs along the south side of our house. We are fortunate to have a two-car garage given the age of our house, so we have a wide expanse facing that sidewalk. A lot of foot traffic goes by on a given day from people going to the store, walking their dogs, or accompanying their children to the bus stop. I wanted something that was more pleasant for them to view.

Realizing that I was on auto-pilot regarding garage colors, I made a practice for a few weeks of walking down alleys and driving alternate ways as I went about work or errands. I was holding a new question and had my eyes open for something that previously was not on my radar screen. I was affirmed that many doors were the exact colors I had been programmed to consider, but I was holding out for something different to inspire me.

Finally, I did see some other colors. More interesting, I saw some garage art. I saw paintings of nature scenes covering entire doors somewhat like public building murals. I assumed that either someone with artistic talents far superior to mine lived there or had paid to get this done. It raised a question for me. "Was I capable of any form of interesting painting?"

I can handle a straight edge quite well, having a steady hand. What could I do on the garage with all straight edges? Silly thoughts crossed my mind like painting each door panel a different color. Then I remembered one garage I had seen that had windows that were shaped to look like a sunset with the rays of the sun spreading across the windows. They weren't painted; carpentry had achieved the effect.

There aren't any windows in our door; it was one big solid expanse. Using masking tape, I created straight edges that would give my door a large sunset with rays. The tape also allowed me to experiment with size and lines before painting. I sanded and painted everything a warm yellow. Once the design was right, I used a deep orange/rust paint to form the sun and the rays and rounded out the sun's edges afterwards.

I was pleased with the result, and it was fun. The comments of neighbors and strangers were gratifying. It gave people something to stop and chat about. I remember quite a few asking me if it was a rising or setting sun. That, in turn, led to interesting conversations. I was walking out to the car one cold, dark, winter, morning when a neighbor who was coming out of the alley, stopped and rolled down her window. She said, "That garage door always brings a smile to my face on dark mornings like this."

Creative Spaces

One of the magical things about a home is its ability to collaborate with you to create spaces for something special. If everything opens to everything else, it is hard to find a spot that focuses your attention and has the intimacy for a meaningful activity. It might be a space in which you feel creative and can work on something you love to do. Or, it might be transforming a space that was meant for one thing into a totally different use. Most of us like a space that is just ours.

Jay Appleton is an English geographer. He argues that we have an ancient human need for what he calls "prospect." This is a spot from which we can see over a considerable distance. Ancient hunter-gatherers needed to look for game and water over a wide vista. Juxtaposed to this, we also need places of "refuge," places we can hide and be safe (perhaps while hunting). These needs are buried in us both for pleasure and survival. Many architects, in particular Frank Lloyd Wright, have perfected the art form of perches and nooks.

Saul and Cathy remodeled their story-and-half home to create a master suite upstairs. They liked the slanted rooflines that afforded a feeling of coziness. Given their city location and limited window options due to the slanted roof, they desired a perch but couldn't see how to have one. Their builder found a solution. They could configure a small patio off the bedroom, just big enough for two. It would be tucked away on the side of the house away from the street. It was both a perch in the treetops and a refuge shrouded by the evergreen boughs that surrounded it. This was mom and dad's space, children not allowed.

Men like their spaces, too. It might be a man cave decorated with a sports theme. For many men, those spaces are often a basement or garage where they can tinker, repair things, fix a car, or build a rabbit hutch. Brian loved to rebuild racecars. When he and his wife built a home in the country, he wanted a large garage with comfort. He heated it, painted the interior, and decorated it

with flags and pennants from car races. Then he added a
big screen television, sofa, and a small refrigerator.

Scott was an artist. He built a small studio in the
wooded acreage behind his home. He also built a multi-
level fort for his son, Pat. It could have almost rivaled
the family fort in *Swiss Family Robinson*. It was built in
such a way that his son could modify it easily to make it
a pirate ship by adding some gangplanks, "cannons," and
a pirate flag. Depending on who came to play, it took on
other appearances as well.

Do you have a space to call your own? Maybe it is
your kitchen when no one else is home. It could be in
your office, if you made a few adjustments. It might be a
small room or even a corner of a room that is your sanctuary where you meditate, journal, or read. The desire
for a space that feels sacred and is tied to meditation or
prayer is increasing. That might be related to changes
that are occurring in people's spiritual lives. For at least
a decade, surveys have found that approximately 40% of
Americans say they attend a religious service weekly, yet
head counts have revealed that actual attendance is about
half of that. I think more people are connecting with
nature, gardens, and their own private sanctuaries, rather
than in the traditional buildings. Perhaps they don't feel
they can admit that at this point in time.

Your child needs a small space as well. My daughter,
Laura, made a closet her small space when she was young.
Even though Laura had her own bedroom, she seemed to
crave smaller spaces. A big box brought hours of pleasure
in the middle of the living room until some event or visitor

necessitated its removal. She equipped it with stuffed animals, a blanket, a snack, and books. She had many books and stuffed animals, way too many animals.

We had a whole zoo by the time she was four. The largest was a pink and white bear that was five feet tall. The smallest was an inch tall zebra. What to do with all of them? Laura did not like the idea of storing them in boxes. That made them too hard to play with. They might not like the dark. They might be lonely without her. A creative solution was needed. Given her interest in small spaces, we had an idea about her closet. It was about four feet deep, four feet wide, and nine feet high.

We agreed to make a home for the stuffed animals that could be a snuggly reading room as well. We lined the whole closet with the stuffed animals from ceiling to floor and added blankets. The final touch was a ceramic, bear-shaped, reading lamp that her godmother had made. Laura helped make harnesses out of yarn for the hanging animals. The four-foot long pterodactyl had its wings spread open over the attic door, so he was ready to take off if the door opened. The pink bear was positioned so Laura could sit in its lap as she read her books. Every animal found its place and seemed content for a number of years.

Connecting the physical softness and comfort of the space with the books created a new association between books, soft animals, and comfort. Sometimes if she was upset with me or with a friend, I would find her in the closet curled up just hugging a book and an animal. She was learning to comfort herself, reflect, and prepare herself to work out whatever it was that had caused her angst.

It also gave her a place to learn to enjoy solitude and quiet. Many children are over-scheduled. There are several trends in American society that encourage this. Despite those pressures, children need the balance of entertaining themselves and having quiet time.

When we decided to stay in our house and create a new home within an existing home, we learned to look at familiar spaces with new eyes. My kitchen was one of those ventures. I had been at a friend's new home and admired her kitchen island and the ability to cook and converse while facing people. That could add to harmony in a home.

Meaningful conversations and physical closeness are the underlying desires behind the trends in kitchen designs, islands, and family rooms that connect to kitchens. We want to be together more on a daily basis. Kitchens are the equivalents of the hearth or the fires of tribal life.

Sadly, at times we get the functional design without the conversations. Rachel Naomi Remen, M.D. offers insight in her book, *Kitchen Table Wisdom*. She says, "When we haven't the time to listen to each other's stories we seek out experts to tell us how to live. The less time we spend together at the kitchen table, the more how-to books appear in the stores and on our bookshelves."

At first I focused on the functional solution—the island—and I was stuck. My floor space and configuration did not have room or any arrangement that could allow for an island. I've learned that when you want something new or feel stuck, let go of the preconceived solution and refocus on the underlying desire. In this case, it was the ability to converse and have eye contact while cooking that mattered, not an island. That helped clarify the hurdle. Creativity needed to happen in the upper spaces of the room, not at the floor level.

We had a table and chairs in the kitchen for my companions. We could hear each other's voices, but no one sat there because of cabinetry. Two cabinets hung from the soffits cutting off visual connectivity between the cooking area and eating area. As I worked at the counter, all I could see was this cabinet. At one time we had considered that a benefit. It gave us more storage space and an eating area that didn't look at pots, pans, and dirty dishes. Now, connectivity was more important.

I tried visualizing the space with the cabinets removed. It seemed like it could have an impact on the whole space. The biggest negative in giving up the cabinets was the lost storage space. That could be solved with some de-cluttering and re-organization. With ideas percolating, I turned to Skip, my house doctor.

He removed the cabinets and reconfigured a door and some shelves. That dealt with the hole that was left after the removal. I gave the cabinets to a friend who wanted storage in her laundry room. The project took one day of Skip's time and one of mine to paint and re-organize.

The impact was even more stellar than I had imagined as shown in the second drawing. The whole room seemed larger and more airy. More light was available from the window in the back door, which had been blocked by the cabinets. Now family or friends could sit and talk or even help out while sitting at the table. The principle of less is more worked in this case. Less storage space had created more space that mattered.

Another type of space is one designed specifically to support your creative endeavors. Those spaces might be permanently arranged rooms or might be temporary spots like a dining room table or a favorite knitting chair. Regardless of the physical location, these all share one thing—they provide a mental/emotional creative space inside of us. A great deal of mental and physical space is allocated this way since an estimated 43 million U.S. households handcrafted items last holiday season. Projects varied from handcrafted gifts to home decor and handmade cards.

The Craft and Hobby Association identifies four main

reasons people craft. The first one they call the value proposition. Crafters weigh the cost of buying versus creating and find they can save money by making things themselves. The second reason is the social factor. Many forms of arts and crafts can be done in groups, so people gather in knitting circles, quilting bees, and scrapbooking groups where they can share ideas, get advice, and spend time with friends and family.

The third one is labeled intrinsic value. This one is about the inner satisfaction of crafting. Completing a quilt or knitting a blanket is not only productive, but it also generates a feeling of satisfaction. If the item is a gift, there is the joy of giving and the delighted response of the recipient as well as the memories that are lasting.

Lastly, there are health benefits to crafting for many of us if we invest the time. Whether painting, sewing, carpentry, knitting, or quilting, doctors often recommend crafts as a way to relieve stress, improve hand-eye coordination, and recover from addiction. It can focus your mind on creating something of beauty, and that lets the worries of the day recede. There's an entire area of medicine called craft therapy.

In *Beauty and the Soul,* author Piero Ferruchi describes a longitudinal study of nine women who began to meet once a week to engage in needlework. Family members were asked to evaluate the women's personality characteristics before the study began and again after a year of the weekly gatherings. The results showed impressive changes. "They showed less anxiety in novel situations, more playfulness, less caution, more capacity to make hard decisions, more independence and vitality, greater ability to show imaginativeness, more capacity to stick to a task, and maintain a goal-directed attitude."

Susan delights in creative Christmas decorations for her tree. She has different theme trees each year. The theme might relate to something special she did that year or a great bargain she discovered. Rotating different sets of ornaments or artificial flowers that she has acquired over the years or regrouping them in a new way to make a different theme all add variety with minimal cost. She also is a good knitter. She knits liners for soldiers' helmets that help keep them warm in winter and cool in summer. She knits about fifty or sixty a year.

Quilting has become increasingly popular. Bev and Jan are both highly skilled and creative. Every son, daughter, grandchild, niece, and nephew wants one of Bev or Jan's prized quilts, tablecloths, or runners. At baby showers, everyone waits in anticipation for the surprise the latest gift will offer.

Like many girls, I learned basic knitting in Girl Scouts. Dishcloths, slippers, and scarves were standard fare. Most of my efforts to learn arts and crafts were for gift giving purposes. Once I had given my family more dishcloths than they could use, I learned to make macramé Christmas trees. When I couldn't think of anyone else who wanted one of them, I tried needlepoint and crewel embroidery. The motivation for me was intrinsic value.

My first few attempts were small. I made macramé hangings and flower pot hangers. When we bought our house, I crafted a needlepoint of "Home Sweet Home."

More needlepoints followed of angels for Laura's bedroom. More recently, for her first wedding anniversary, I created a cross-stitch commemorating the date of the wedding. My greatest satisfaction came from making a crewel embroidery.

A wonderful wildflower embroidery pattern inspired me. I knew my mother-in-law would love it. The only problem was that it was 40" x 18" and that seemed huge to me. Given I would have three-fourths of a year before Christmas, I decided to go for it. I finished just in time. Then, we had it framed for her. After hanging in her home for about 30 years, it came back to us after her death. It now hangs in our guest bedroom reminding us of her love of flowers and the ivy she started from my wedding bouquet.

Crafting is a delightful way to beautify your own home, as well as other's, discover creative juices that you might otherwise never sample, and experience hours of pleasure in the process of preparing a lasting gift for someone you love.

Moving Beauty

Sometimes we get bored with our homes. If everything is working, we just fall into patterns of forgetfulness. We stop appreciating them. A little of the magic or life goes out of them. Homes can teach us something about relationships.

Our homes need attention even when everything is fine. We can add some new energy without spending a penny. One way to do this, and get the added benefit of some exercise, is to move things around. You can move curtains, throws, and pillows. Once you start moving your body around your home, you start noticing just how many other things you can move. It's good exercise as well.

Ellen has one specific area of interest; it's the artwork that hangs on her walls. She moves them around by season or by her mood. You can move family photos or any other accessories that you have. Moving plants can be fun as long as you remember each plant's light requirements.

Or, you can go big time. You can move the FURNI-TURE. I remember being very antsy one night when my family had gone to a basketball game many years ago. I wanted to transform the living room. My sofa's location is fixed, given that I don't have any other wall that is long enough for it, but I could move all the chairs, my antique desk, and my standing lamps. I had a great time trying one configuration after another. My lovely antique desk found a new home under our wall clock in the dining room. I added a tall vase from a trip. Chairs were reconfigured, and I switched the rug that was in the sunroom with the one in front of the fireplace.

I put a sign on the back door telling Bob and Laura they had to enter through the front door. I wanted them to get the full effect and I wanted to see their faces. Subsequently, Laura told me that when they saw the sign, they had just looked at each other and said, "Mom's been at it again. What will it be this time? She's only had a few hours."

They approved of what I had done. They said the room felt different. I laughed as they moved around and sat in different chairs. They reminded me of Goldilocks in *The Three Bears*. Moving three chairs, one desk, and three standing lamps had revitalized the room. I noticed that we spent more time in that room for a while after that.

You can move almost anything. Moving the air in a room with an attractive ceiling fan will provide comfort and reduced air-conditioning bills. Rooms might be able to trade curtains. Bring home unique stones from a trip, and put them in a small woven basket. Move a colorful scarf or blanket that was sitting in a chest, and throw it over the back of a sofa or chair. Collect all your favorite framed photos from shelves, chests, and drawers and mount them on a stairway or in a special spot so you have a gallery.

In a 1994 survey on homes, the question was asked, "If you could add a room, which room would you most want to add?" A library was the top choice. Libraries speak to our thirst for knowledge, time to read and reflect, and a sense of calm. These are high priorities for Sally, but her home did not have room for a library, and she did not have money for an addition.

She already had many bookcases, and some books were still boxed in the basement. She brainstormed with some friends. They had trouble understanding her problem. It seemed as if she just needed another bookcase or two or should clean out her books and give some away. As her friends asked questions, she talked about the benefits of a library. She wished her books could surround her. She wanted to be able to see them, not have them scattered all over the house.

One of her friends finally said, "Maybe you could see this differently. You love your books like companions. They are your friends, so you want them to surround you. I think you've already begun doing that by having them surround the whole house. Think of the whole house as a library. Move more of the books out of the bookcases or the boxes. Move more of your favorite books into the living room, which is where you read the most. Set them up as decorative stacks on shelves or on your wide windowsills. You could do that in other rooms as well. Then you could see them and experience them differently than when they are in the bookcases. And it moves them out of the boxes."

Sally got her big "aha" in that moment. Thinking of the whole house as a library was a new idea. She loved the idea of incorporating the books into the rooms and out of the bookcases. The next time her friends came over, they had the grand tour of the new house-wide library. Many books had moved to new homes. The most prominent books were leather bound or tabletop books with wonderful photography. Her small collection of antique books had a particularly visible spot on the fireplace mantel well away from any danger from the fire.

We are creatures of habit in our physical and non-physical dimensions. Think about how we develop habits in our relationships and let them go stale, just as we do with our homes. Shaking up some habits and adding variety and surprises back into our relationships will strengthen and renew them.

Possibilities Are Quiet

I was frustrated with a long-time problem. It came up over and over for years and was a source of disagreement in my family. Strange, how something as simple as a door can be so annoying. At other times it is so welcoming that the contrast irritated me that much more.

In this case, we were dealing with an interior door that wasn't welcoming. We were balancing the conflicting needs for light, warmth, cold, privacy, beauty, and money. We each had our priorities. We'd have a discussion, vote, and retreat to our corners with varying emotions; the only shared emotion was frustration that we were covering the same ground again.

My home faces west. The Native American spiritual tradition identifies the four sacred directions in the book, *The Sacred Tree*. The West is associated with darkness. The authors describe it this way, "The West is the direction from which darkness comes. It is the direction of the unknown, of going within, of dreams, of prayer and of meditation. The West is the place of testing, where the will is stretched to its outer limits so that the gift of perseverance can be won."

Since thunder and lightning also tend to be part of the West, they symbolically represent learning to manage power in a harmonious way. It might be to use power to heal, to see, to understand, to create harmony. These are critical lessons in the development of human will power. I didn't know this during the years that I was trying to tackle the problem of the door.

We are grateful that we face west during the winter.

Although darkness comes early, there is wonderful light in late afternoon. The sun plays upon our home's cream-colored stucco exterior. The stucco receives the warmth and draws it in. Light rays enter the two windows in the west facing living room, dance around, and flow beyond into the dining room. Between the windows, however, reigned darkness.

The entrance is an unheated foyer that opens into the living room through a solid oak door. Fortunately, in the winter, the door is always closed between the foyer and living room blocking out the cold. Unfortunately, it also blocks out the light from the foyer windows and the windows in the exterior door.

Aesthetically and energetically, I had a problem. I love all the wood in our home, but a solid piece of oak measuring roughly 7' x 4' in the middle of the wall just didn't seem right. It loomed over the room, especially at night. It created a solid, thick darkness. The living room was asking for more light and something else that I couldn't name.

I tried to name it. For years I tried. Is the door dissatisfaction related to the larger desire to have a porch across the whole front of the house rather than just the foyer? A vote nixed that due to the cost. In addition, a porch would reduce the light from the two windows.

The starting question was, "What should we do with that door?" Questions usually lead to other questions, and frequently, they are the either/or types of questions. Remove the door entirely or leave it open in the winter? Which do we want—the heat or the light? Are we willing to pay the costs of heating the foyer?

Either/ors lead to lists of tradeoffs or pros and cons. If the door was left open, then the living room heat would warm the foyer at quite a price. Removing the door would have the negative effect of losing any privacy between strangers at the outer door and our living areas. Bob and Laura felt that while light would be nice, the heat and privacy were more important, so continue to keep the door closed.

Life goes on. Other things compete for attention. Then something wakes us up again. Since there doesn't seem to be a solution or significant need, the issue gets dismissed or forgotten. The power of habit takes over. We develop a coat of armor around the issue, and it becomes harder to even notice the inner promptings. Sometimes this works to our advantage but usually not.

After a particularly gray November, December, January, and February in Minnesota, I had had enough. My home wanted a new question, a more complex question, an "and" question rather than either/or, yes or no. The one that worked was an integrative question, "Is there any configuration that retains privacy, doesn't waste heat, and provides light?" Those elements spelled out my ideal requirements and enabled me to stop looking at the current door. It gave me a vision quest instead of a problem.

The obvious then struck. The exterior door had windows. That door gave privacy, it closed out the exterior cold, and it provided the opening for light. The vision of an interior door with a window materialized. Hope began to emerge. Excitement replaced frustration. It's strange how some things have such a long gestation period.

Human beings need space to be creative beings before they start doing things. Let the ideas percolate. Move into "flow." Browse through favorite related books. Playing with ideas about modifying the door to include a glass insert invited the unnamed desire to emerge. My home and I wanted beauty as well as our other needs. The souls of people and homes crave beauty.

Bob and I had always wished we had the right place for stained glass. At local art fairs we always stopped to admire such works of beauty. Could this be the long desired spot? I engaged Bob with my vision. He didn't ask any of the questions I expected. The vision of stained glass touched something in him as well. He liked the idea and began measuring and bringing his engineer's eye to the questions of the weight of glass and size of the opening we should create. It was the beginning of a fun and satisfying project for both of us.

We found the right expert to work with us. The cost of $800 was not prohibitive, but it was enough to give pause. We decided that this was going to be our Christmas present to each other. Next year would be our 30th wedding anniversary, so mark the year with something special. That decision added more meaning to this collaborative effort, which was already much more fun and romantic than our usual approach in which he plays a less active role.

The design engaged both of our strengths. I am good at seeing new opportunities and have a sense of design. He brings good taste, detailed attention to measurements and weight. I tend to eyeball things, and he measures to

a sixteenth of an inch. Air meets Earth, one could say. We have a stained glass lamp and chandelier that we had purchased over the years. I suggested we use them as a source of inspiration for design and color. All the pieces of the puzzle of the design, colors, and size fell into place like magic. Three days before Christmas, our designer delivered it. The new piece filled the upper portion of the door providing the light of a widow, yet we still had warmth and privacy.

As I descend the stairs each morning, it is the first thing I see. It invites a lightness of spirit and is a constant reminder of the wonder of creative endeavors. By adding a new light in the foyer ceiling, we can experience light and beauty even at night as we curl up and stay awhile. That is an added joy. For those who enter our home, it is a unique welcoming signpost of beauty, balance, and integration.

My home has taught me the lessons of the West – persistence, will, and harmonious power. The window has added meaning because the birthing process was long and thoughtful. The possibilities were there, waiting quietly, until we found the right question that would open up a new flow of thought. The right questions are somewhat similar to fertilizer; they help jump-start growth. Our one act had fulfilled so many desires that I learned lifetime lessons about the critical importance of asking the right question, providing space for creativity, and solving problems with simple beauty and subtle harmony. The physical nature of home is as much about soul, spirit, and relationships as it is about things. Life likes to tease us into experiencing this.

~

Reflections/Suggestions for Another Day:

• How could you play with your home to uncover beauty?

• How do your play with your family or friends?

• What is your attitude toward restrictions?

• How can you shift it to see restrictions as possibilities?

• What special spaces exist in your home that meet the needs of each person for their own space and for creative space?

• What kinds of spaces would be good for your home to have or to enhance?

• Have you had success in moving beauty? Describe it and appreciate yourself for your creativity.

• What things could you move to achieve your goals?

• Do you have quiet possibilities waiting for you to give them voices?

• Design a plan to do something about one of these using any of the other exercises in this book.

• Explore the resurgence of do-it-yourself projects. See www.curbly.com.

Infused with Stories

Poet Muriel Rukeyser tells us "the universe is made of stories, not atoms." What does she mean? She's not telling us that science is wrong. She's telling us how we create meaning out of facts and experiences. Stories are the way we give meaning and wholeness to life; they are like a completed puzzle. The stories can be huge, such as *The Universe is A Green Dragon: A Cosmic Creation Story* by cosmologist Brian Swimme, or they can be small, such as how you came to have your name. Rukeyser could also have said that home is made of stories, not wood and stone.

The oral tradition of storytelling goes back to ancient times and is part of all cultures. Those stories were particularly important because that was how knowledge and culture were passed on to the next generation. In addition, a good tale made sense of the world, provided examples of the right way to live, honored the gods, and was entertaining. Those few primitive cultures that did not tell stories were the first to die out.

Where did you get your images of home, family, and your identity? Certainly the stories of your childhood experiences of house and home have a lasting impact. Often your stories include more than your own home such as the homes of grandparents, other relatives, or friends. It might also include the houses you were never invited to enter and the lasting impressions that made. Your stories form your understanding of your personal universe.

The legends, fairy-tales, and narratives we read in books or that are sung to us in songs and ballads sink deep into our consciousness as well. Stories have a way of imprinting themselves into your mind more than do facts, logic, and analysis; that is why they are so powerful. Their effect is subtle, so it can take effort to notice what has lodged itself in your psyche. Storytellers often became powerful shamans, priests, judges, and rulers. Some studies suggest that people who read books are happier than those who do not because of the power of stories.

Becoming Human

The sharing of stories is the most fundamental way to become human, to grow loving lasting relationships, and to impart wisdom. Home is where we tell our stories and learn who we are or want to be. It is also where we learn to evaluate and reject what is not good for us as the wealth of generational wisdom is handed-down through stories.

We tell many kinds of stories. Until you have a well-developed inner life, the stories you tell or hear are about action outside of yourself. It is the story of the hunt or the raiding of the village or the rescue of the sheep from the wolf.

The inner life arises in the privacy of our thoughts, unseen and inaccessible to outsiders. These stories are fundamentally different. The individual creates the characters, the action, and most importantly the meaning. These stories carry dreams of what kind of person we want to be, who we want to spend our life with, and how we see ourselves fitting into the world.

If the nature of our approach to housing and homes is a concrete demonstration of the development of something as intangible as our consciousness, certainly our daily lives are a manifestation of the stories of both our personal consciousness and that of the collectives within which we grow—our families, friends, neighborhoods, and nations.

Homes are infused with stories. If you live long enough in one place, the day will come when it is difficult to find things in the home that do not have a story. Even the wall by the basement steps tells a story; if you look closely enough, there may still be the faint lines that measured a child's growth year by year. Even if you are young, there are many stories inside of you influencing every decision as you set up your home.

That old-fashioned armchair was grandma and grandpa's first purchase after they had Uncle Joe. The closet in the front office was once a playroom. The vase recalls the 30th anniversary trip to Greece. The collection of shells in a basket speaks of hours on the shores of Sanibel Island from a vacation last year. If the furniture could speak, especially the tables, they could tell stories from hundreds of conversations—sad, glad, confused, triumphant, silly, and touching.

Some stories keep adding new chapters. Bob surprised me with an unpainted rocker the first Christmas after we were married. I thoroughly enjoyed watching the beautiful grains emerge as the stain seeped in, and the whole rocker came to life as its natural gifts appeared. We became connected. Years later I rocked in it for hours during the early stages of labor before our daughter's birth and then for more years rocked her to sleep in it. It still sits in a place of honor in my living room imbued with memories.

Your home has a story as well. If you learn it, you will know more about your neighborhood, city, and history. A home will help you remember who you are and why nurturing each other matters, even when you are struggling. A quiet evening stroll, with stops in various rooms, will bring back vivid memories with wisdom to help you through the day.

BJ's home is a treasure trove for the most meaningful items that have marked her life's journey, items she has purchased because she loved them, or they held the meaning of an experience. Other bits and pieces, she literally picked up on a beach. Many things were gifts with some passed down from ancestral hands. In all cases, she says, "Those most cherished items hold the synergy of much more than the item itself. I have long been a lover of the story and the meaning behind the object."

We invite people into our homes because we want our home to speak to the visitor, and tell them a bit about us that we might be too self-conscious to put into words. A home is a hub of frequent conversations and less frequently, but more meaningfully, of dialog. Your home can provide a support system of meaning that holds you during dialog as you share dreams that may challenge your current lifestyle or work to understand contrary views that are leading to strife.

Sharing dinner is an ideal time for telling the stories of the day. It is one of the most ancient social activities on earth. In *Kitchen Table Wisdom: Stories That Heal,* Rachel Naomi Remen describes how important this is: "Everybody is a story. When I was a child, people sat around kitchen tables and told their stories. We don't do that so much anymore. Sitting around the table telling stories is not just a way of passing time. It is the way the wisdom gets passed along. The stuff that helps us to live a life worth remembering."

I wrote my first book, *Who We Could Be at Work*, in 1994. It was a business book about ethics and values in creating a meaningful and healthy workplace. I was surprised at how many people from CEOs to union officials, told me how much they learned at the dinner table about values, leadership, and work. In a home, eating meals is one of the greatest binding rituals we can perform. We aren't just feeding our stomachs. We are nurturing the mind, heart, and soul of everyone at the table.

If each person has a turn to describe the day, a pattern is established that lasts for a lifetime. We are telling our own life stories a chapter a day. Older siblings can reassure younger ones, that they, too, went through some trauma of embarrassment and survived. We watch each other grow and learn how to deal with values, conflict, goals, and disappointments through the modeling and discussions with those we trust. As children grow into teens, the patterns can help keep communication open through the challenging years. Friends can share as well, helping each other through the ups and downs of life.

There are other times that are good for storytelling. Holidays bring back memories that are shared as a tree is decorated, or pumpkins carved, or as a flag is raised. Emily has two boys who are active in sports. They spend hours in the car each week. She decided to prohibit electronic diversions in the car. The ritual of sharing events from the day or discussing the news became part of the car ride.

Bedtime is a great storytelling time for children. Depending on their age, the nature of the stories may change. The stories might be fantasies if they are quite young. By middle school, fables with morals or stories about when they were very young are well received, as well as childhood stories about mom and dad or a grandparent. Teaching children to tell their own stories about themselves, as early and regularly as possible, also will help them through the teen years.

Janice began to notice that her son, Jason, was withdrawing, as he got older. School activities meant he was missing at dinner more frequently. Weekends he was with his friends. She reflected on how they used to read together in bed and how he loved to talk; she and her husband, Bruce, would have to carry him off to his bedroom as he continued to jabber away. What had happened? she wondered.

Bruce and Janice talked about this change. Bruce felt it was just a normal part of growing up. He pointed out that no guy wanted to sit in bed with his mom and spill his guts. Bruce's comment led Janice to realize that the change had started very slowly about the time Jason was ten. The conversations had continued, but he had started making her come and sit on the side of his bed.

Then a few years later, he had ended that practice by asserting he wasn't a little kid that needed to be put to bed. Janice wanted to find a way to renew the conversations that fit who Jason was now.

Bedtime still seemed like the only time of the day that she could count on all of them being home. She and Bruce were in the habit of reading in bed before going to sleep. If she could just get Jason in the room, she was sure they could renew their communication. They were still close, and Jason wasn't rejecting them; he just seemed to be slipping away. She decided to add a chair and ottoman to their bedroom, one big enough for Jason's lanky frame.

Then, she waited for nights when she knew that Jason had had something important going on—a big test, the delivery of the latest edition of the school paper that he edited, or a soccer match. Then she or Bruce would call out to Jason and ask him about the event. It was natural for him to fall into the chair as the answers and further questions continued. A new pattern began to emerge that included his initiating conversations. Janice always thanked that chair for helping to make the invitation agreeable for Jason.

Tables are important places for conversations—kitchen

tables, coffee tables, and dining room tables. While the death of the dining room has been announced, I doubt that is the whole truth. It is apparent in new homes, but the majority of people I talk to who live in older homes with pleasant dining rooms, still love them and use them. They are places for any dinner that is a little special, for homework, for spreading out the tax materials, and for craft projects and games, but most importantly for conversations.

I have been a member of a group that fondly calls itself, the potluck group. We were all high school teachers in the same school when we were young. After thirty-six years we are still together. We alternate among our homes every month, except July and August, for dinner with each person bringing part of the meal. We've traded help, experiences, recipes, clothes, and woven our lives together. We've talked, laughed, debated, cried, and advised each other while sitting around our respective dining room tables.

Jerry and Lynnette recently added a dining room to their home. It was designed around a cherry table that can seat up to eighteen people. They love to entertain their large extended family. The room has many kinds of wood in it because Lynnette and her husband wanted it to remind them of a forest. The windows look out onto a park with many trees that feel as if they are part of their home.

Our homes, with all their furnishings, rituals, yards, and their extensions, such as cars, provide assistance in telling us stories about ourselves—who we are and who we want to be—as well as providing a venue that encourages those conversations. They can help us become the best possible humans, if we work together.

Mapping Your Conversation Centers

• Make a rough map of each floor of your house.

• Take a walk through each space and note on your map every conversation center.

• After you have completed the whole house, write down your conclusions about the quantity, variety, and distribution of those centers.

• Ask yourself if you are satisfied with the types and distribution of the centers.

• Then ask yourself how frequently the spaces are used for conversation.

• Assess if you are happy with the quality of the conversations.

• Record any of these answers.

• Decide if anything needs to be enhanced and how to do it.

Know Thyself

When we can tell a story that reveals who we are to others or even to ourselves, we deepen and strengthen self-knowledge. Meaningful homes want us to be the playwright as well as the main characters. Advertisers have become so effective, they are becoming the playwrights, and we may become only the characters. The effect may be a short-term pride and delight in our rooms and houses rather than long-term happiness.

Wouldn't knowing ourselves be the easiest thing in the

world to do? Actually, it is difficult to know yourself. The Oracle at Delphi in Ancient Greece was sought out by many to inquire into a diversity of issues including the meaning of life. One of the statements particularly associated with the Oracle's wisdom was the admonishment, "Know Thyself."

Which "you" is the real one? What color do you love regardless of the current styles? Do you know when you have chosen something beautiful because it speaks to something innate in you? The earlier we learn these lessons, the more happiness with staying power we will have. Self-knowledge and enriching experiences help strengthen us to stand against the herd mentality and social pressures that are to come.

When our daughter, Laura, was about to turn six and start kindergarten, she had a significant opportunity to learn about creating beauty from the inside out. We arranged for a rite of passage experience. We told her she could move into the larger, brighter guest room and decorate it. She was thrilled since she loved art and considered this a big art project.

We started with the hard work of creating her "canvas." The room was wallpapered with seven layers. Laura couldn't use a steamer, but she could help bag the paper and wash some of the glue off the walls. She liked discovering what the different layers looked like. She made up stories about who lived in the room with each layer.

Laura was getting tired of the work by the time we reached the original walls. The deep purple color revived her interest as she imagined what color she wanted in her room. Dad had the fun idea of taking white primer and painting big fun characters on the walls as we prepped them.

The rules for her new venture were an important piece that would take some time to sink in. They included some budget limits, as well as process steps to help her select good ideas from not so good ones, and how to test ideas before implementing them. First, she had a dream stage during which she painted or drew lots of possibilities in her idea notebook. That helped her consider her own ideas before seeing the store models of children's rooms.

To narrow down the ideas, we asked what she loved most and would continue to love for a number of years. Laura's favorite book and movie featured a unicorn, so we found a wallpaper border featuring these lovely creatures. Two weeks after taping a large sample to the wall, she was still enthused about it and had decided it should go around at the ceiling level. It seemed that we were now on easy street.

I suggested that the walls could be white or a color out of the border. Once the painting was done, then, we could move on to the bedspread and other accessories. Laura thought white paint would be good, but all white would be boring. She wanted something more on the walls. The difficulty was she couldn't define "more." That was frustrating. We closed the door of the room for a little while.

About a week later, she had discovered her answer. "I know what I want in my bedroom." She paused before making her announcement. "I want the world. We are going to paint things from all over the world on different walls. I want the Sphinx and a pyramid and some Egyptian people like the pharaoh. Another spot could have a castle like Europe. Some dolphins and the island of Hawaii would be great fun. Let's see, I like Korean ladies and temples. Then we will have some Native Americans and a pueblo. When can we start?"

I was dumbfounded and said, "You're only going on six. How do you know about all these things?" She considered that. "You talk about the world all the time, especially, when you are with Aunt Pat. I saw the pueblos when we went to New Mexico. I want to paint my own pictures, not buy them."

I would have preferred to buy them. I have no talent when it comes to painting these kinds of images, and I wasn't sure what a room painted by a six-year-old would look like. I admitted that to her, but it didn't faze her a bit. "I want to do it; it's my room. You just need to help a little." Bob and I talked about how we had intended for this to be her learning experience. Could we stay true to that?

Like any good playwright, she noticed which scenes were working and which weren't and tried again. After a couple of false starts, she found her Egyptian paper doll book to show me what she had in mind. We realized we could make them into stencils. They worked so well she thought we should create homemade stencils for the major elements of the other drawings. I contributed the idea of masking tape after we had trouble with paper stencils. We had fun working together. The room was delightful. More important was Laura's pleasure and

pride in designing a room that was truly hers. She told the
story of the room to everyone she knew. The story told
her things about herself.

A funny thing happened a year later. Our parish
Catholic school was going through a consolidation, and
we were looking for another school. I discovered a new
Waldorf School and the more I learned, the more I liked.
Unfortunately, I was told, her grade level might be full,
but the teacher agreed to consider us.

Mr. Stevens showed up promptly at our home and
focused his attention on Laura. One of the things he
asked her was what she had done that excited her and
made her proud. She immediately wanted him to come
and see her bedroom. He stared at her room and listened
as she talked about it. By the time we got back down-
stairs, he turned to me and said, "I don't need to ask
much more. Laura's story and bedroom tell me she and
Waldorf would be a good match."

The power of someone else's story often teaches lessons

to others as well as to the storyteller. Laura learned all the things we had expected. We learned more about the inner world and consciousness of our daughter and about parenting. We had stayed true to the intent of the project, even when we were concerned about the outcome. And that bedroom helped her get into a school that had an enormously positive impact on her life.

It was several years later that an additional insight came to me about how a home helps parent a child. One night as I wandered through my home considering some new touch to add, an "aha" moment came. There, on my living room walls, was my "room with the world on it." There was the painting of the Great Wall of China over the fireplace, Ancient Greece over the sofa, a papyrus print over the desk, and two small paintings of English cottages over the water fountain. I had not consciously decided to put the world on my walls; I learned something about my inner consciousness. I think those images had also unconsciously slipped into Laura's consciousness.

Visual Stories

Stories can be told without words. Art arises out of stories. Ancient cave drawings tell stories, teach about the hunt, and worship the spirit world. Those who are artistic share their tales though paintings, drawings, and pottery bowls. Photography is another means that is accessible to more of us. I don't mean photography as in knowledge of lenses, F-stops, and camera specifications. I mean the pleasure of crafting a memorable photo, especially one that tells a story.

It takes thoughtfulness to understand what types of photos speak to you. There are awe-inspiring shots—frequently of nature. There are memory-recording photos as in vacation shots or baby pictures. Occasionally, we need documentation photos that capture belongings and a house at a specific moment. These get stored in safety deposit boxes for insurance purposes. You might want to reflect on how you would categorize your photos.

Most photos tell a slice of a story, perhaps a momentary scene in a much larger story that the picture cannot tell. We capture the slice in a sentence. That was the day John graduated. That was your first bike. What a lovely sunset shot.

The visual story is different. It is a photo with elements that invoke a sense of time passing, characters, and intrigue. It calls to you to stop and read the story, not just look at the image. Perhaps there is a picture of your grandmother in the dress she wore to your wedding. She is seated next to a table with a vase of red roses. Standing upright, next to the vase, is a sheet of marbled vellum paper. The names of all the other deceased grandparents are recorded in calligraphy. It is the expression on her face, as she gazes at the list, which speaks of the past and the future.

It's easy to take many pictures, especially with digital cameras. The hard part is organizing and displaying them so that you can see and recall what moved you. You don't have access to the stories when they are in the box or were never developed.

Well-organized photos in chronological order in

albums can make for hours of viewing enjoyment. The story then arises from the series of the photos. The album for the year tells a long story. Many people do not have the time or discipline, though, to do that. The newer digital frames could become your new album. Keep one media card per year, and slip it into the digital frame for your photo night review.

A historical framed family gallery on a wall in the family room, hall, or stairway may be viable alternatives. The large collage frames are handy for this. You don't have to change those pictures very often or perhaps not at all if you have room to keep adding to it. Pianos and mantels are other spots for display. Now there are also web based photo albums. So there are more options that are easier to use.

My older cousin did research about our family history and found pictures from our childhood and previous generations. We have all found these of value and wanted copies. It's fun and forms bonds when we see this next generation's baby pictures and see how much they look like other older or deceased relatives.

Photography is one way of keeping the living and the dead remembered and honored. Video cameras offer another experience that brings sound and action into the story, but they aren't viewed as often.

Once in a while, a room can be decorated in such a way that it tells a story. Marge had significant water damage in her downstairs bathroom from a leak in the main stack. A large area of sheet rock around the sink and doorway needed to be torn out and replaced. This presented an opportunity for redecorating their down-stairs bathroom. Marge and her two boys, Dan and Sam, five and seven years of age respectively, decided to do something special.

They spent some time talking about options. The boys love to swim, and they live on a lake so they quickly settled on a water theme. They decided against doing a tropical fish theme because this was already so popular in many people's bathrooms.

In the process of these discussions, Marge's artistic friend, Cathy, volunteered to help. She suggested a fishing theme, and they loved the idea. The boys and their mom went to the library to find books with pictures of fish native to their area. Marge painted the walls a beautiful blue color. Cathy helped gently whitewash the walls to develop the water effect.

The collaborative effort led to a bathroom that told the story of a boy fishing on a lazy summer day, as well as of the underwater world of the fish in the lake. Waves gently splashed on a beach close to the ceiling line and white puffy clouds above that floated in the summer sky. The boy fishing in a boat was catching a summer nap. His fishing line was tied to his toe as his foot leaned over the edge of the boat.

Below the waterline, Dan and Sam added brightly colored fish inspired by the book pictures but colored by their imaginations. There were also strands of painted seaweed waving in the water, a crayfish, and rocks just on top of the baseboards. They painted an anchor with a chain that wound its way down the wall to sit on the bottom of the lake. Bubbles coming out of the fish's mouth completed the walls. The floor was redone with textured sand tiles. A fishing net served as window dressing.

The boys were proud of their work and loved showing off their story. Marge's greatest delight is telling the story of the discovery of the deeper well of creative ideas inside her sons and how the experience raised their self-esteem and gave them a 'can do' type of experience.

Changing Inner Stories

A home accompanies you as your life continues. With the changes in your story, the home changes. A divorce may require a major overhaul of the home or even needing to leave it. A baby frequently leads to the complete redecorating of a room and alterations throughout the house for safety, warmth, and new activities in old rooms. Sometimes we need to explore our inner stories before we are able to change our dwellings.

Renee was an only child. Not long after her dad died, it became clear that her mom, Liz, needed a change in her dwelling space, but everything else was unclear. One day Liz could not bear the thought of leaving her dear home. The next day, she didn't feel she could stay in the house. She did not want an apartment—too many noisy strangers. An independent living facility was out of the question—I'm not that old. Liz was also worried about money. This indecisiveness was unlike her mother, so after months of not getting any clear answers, Renee sought insight from her Aunt Violet, her mom's older sister.

Her aunt demurred at first, but with prodding and a promise of confidentiality, she finally explained. Renee's mom was deeply conflicted. She wanted to stay in the house and have Renee come back home, but she was afraid to ask. Renee did not understand why her mother couldn't talk to her about all of this.

"I think your mom is caught in a sad family story," Aunt Violet told Renee. "When we were young, our grandma, your great-grandmother, came to live with us. Our parents felt they had to take her in. Things did not go well. Your grandmother and great-grandmother fought constantly and said some very regrettable things to each other. The ensuing silence was even worse as they hardly spoke for several years until she died. Your mom is afraid of that story repeating itself. If she tells you what she is stewing about, then you might agree to something you don't want out of a sense of obligation."

After talking to friends and a counselor, Renee had a plan to replace her mom's old story with a new one. Renee suggested that they finish off her mom's partially renovated lower level. Renee would become a renter in her childhood home. Mom could continue living independently on the main floor. Renee, who had a dog and traveled a couple times a month, would have someone to care for the dog and could enjoy a home-cooked meal once a week.

Her mom was delighted. Renee's story, of how things could be, helped replace Liz's story of the past. Then they could change their home to fit new needs and relationship. Her mom refused rent, but they reached a compromise.

They also agreed on an annual review of the situation knowing that either or both of their needs could change.

Sometimes you need to do your inner work without another person. In those cases, consider enlisting the help of your home. Perhaps you have lost a partner or a job. Maybe you are bored or frustrated about something. Your inner stories are essentially spiritual stories giving meaning to whatever is happening in your world, whether it is physical or emotional. When you engage the story with your imagination and your physical world, you increase the odds significantly that you will fashion greater happiness. One of those times for me was when Laura started college and moved into the dorm.

In the midst of the flurry of excitement for her, Bob and I were a little sad, as we completed all the activity needed for an entering college freshman. Logically, it didn't seem like we should be sad. She would just be across the river. It wasn't as if she was going far away.

This was the first big physical marker of her journey out of our home into creating a home of her own in the world. College, new job, marriage, and home of her own—we felt it all in this first step. For Laura, it was another rite of passage. Bob dealt with it internally. The story I was telling myself was about loss. I needed a physical rite of passage for me. I turned to my home.

I did not want to touch her bedroom; that would really cause me to feel her loss. It would also have bothered Laura. Practically speaking, I knew she would be home for holidays, some weekends, and maybe decide not to continue dorm life.

We have a bedroom that was being used partly as a guest bedroom and partly as Laura's study space. This could be an opportunity. The student-sized desk we had assembled when she was in third grade was too small for her now. The sleepovers with Grandma had ended when she moved into assisted living so having a guest bed was less important. The room was ready to be reborn.

I started writing a dialog imagining that the room was asking the questions. I was answering. This is just one example of how to use your imagination to fit your own situation.

Q. What do you believe you are losing?

A. Our daily conversations, her physical presence, basically all the time we spend together.

Q. So, you want to spend time with me?

A. Yes, I will feel better if I can stop thinking about loss and instead find something positive for me in her leaving. Making this room mine might be a way to do that.

Q. Isn't having more free time a blessing?

A. If you put it that way, then yes, but a mixed blessing.

Q. What could we do together?

A. One of my favorite pastimes is reading.

Q. There are many places in the house to read. Is there something different I can offer to make it a better or different reading space?

A. Good question. Yes, we could make you more like a library. Being surrounded by books always comforts and inspires me.

Q. Why is that?

A. When I lost my parents and my friends when I was little, I spent a lot of my free time at the library reading. It filled a big void. It let me into the characters' lives.

Q. Do you want to move all your books in here? You have a lot of books.

A. No, I just want the fiction books. The business books belong in the office.

Q. I know libraries have bookshelves and books. What else would be important?

A. A comfortable chair with a foot-stool, a blanket to wrap in on cool evenings, a good reading lamp, the book-cases, and books.

Q. Is there anything else you would want to do in here? I am an adaptable space.

A. Spend some time with Bob and listen to music.

Q. So how can that be incorporated into me?

A. (After talking to Bob) Buy a computer and desk for Bob so that I can read, and he can be on the computer. We could move the stereo system in here as well.

As the conversation continued, I developed a plan about painting, buying a new rug, and adding pictures on the wall. I was feeling better already. Once Laura was settled in school, I used my free time to implement my plan with the agreement of my family. Instead of feeling sad, I was having fun for the next month as I created my new dream space.

Changing our inner stories can also require profound life-long work. Antonio feels rooted in New Mexico, even though Minnesota has been his home most of his life. As he tells it, each place contributes something different to his life and healing. His childhood life in the 1940s in New Mexico was rich in love but was also a story of poverty and discrimination in many areas of life. The white parents of a girl that he liked would not allow her to go to prom with him, despite her protests.

Antonio was taught early in life that education was important, and he should become more than a laborer. He did that and ended up with a good job in Minnesota. His life here allows him a cerebral opportunity to reflect on what occurred in his childhood, so he achieves an intellectual understanding that opens the door to the healing process. To actually heal, he needs to return to his roots in New Mexico so that the emotional memories come flooding back, and things inside are stirred up. Then he can complete the healing of his inner stories on both levels.

I believe there is a lesson there for all of us. It certainly was true for me the first time I returned to my childhood home. The physical reality and intangible memories affect us differently so sometimes we need both experiences for deep healing.

Critter Stories

We've looked at animals as part of physical and emotional beauty. Now, let's look at them through a different lens. Many people love animal stories. The stories aren't just cute; they offer insight and meaning about human beings. Helen lived on two acres on the outskirts of town. She had decided to pursue writing full-time and thought a nature-filled living space would inspire her. She, also, wanted to spend more time gardening. In particular, she wanted a large rose garden. The moving party her friends had surprised her with included gifts of many rose bushes.

She planted them with care and was rewarded with dozens of blossoms, but that didn't last long. A deer and a young fawn had found the delicious treat. Helen stood at her window that first early morning of her sighting as she prepared to dash out and shoo them away. Then a shift occurred. She quietly stole down the stairs to a better viewing spot until the deer left of their own accord.

Later, she told one of her friends about the incident. He immediately offered to build a fence. "No," she said. "I realized, watching them inspires me more than anything else I do. I'm content to return their gift with a gift of some of my roses." Animals can inspire us.

Professor Yi-Fu Tuan is a Chinese-American geographer famous for pioneering the field of human geography and merging it with philosophy, art, psychology, and religion. He is known as a humanist geographer. In his many years of teaching at universities in Toronto, Minnesota, and Wisconsin, he has delved into pets and owners as well as many other diverse areas.

He says, "We humans are compelled to love creatures unlike us because we were and are totally dependent on them. Domestication is a long-drawn-out and often cruel procedure. Nevertheless, in its early stages, we humans had to treat the animals we wished to domesticate with tender, loving care.

"Another factor is our need to see our virtues vividly. Animals, serving as metaphors, answer that need. Thus the dog stands undeviatingly for loyalty, the cat for independence, the horse for elegance, the tiger for power, the lion for nobility, and the panda for cuteness."

We also associate ourselves with animals because they have intelligence and can learn. That intelligence may be different from a human's, but it is there. Whales, dolphins, birds, chimps, and other animals have been taught to communicate with humans. They also have emotions and exhibit virtues. Some animals seem to be able to alert people when seizures are coming on. If you have ever risen in the middle of the night for a good cry, chances are it was your dog that curled up next to you offering comfort. These are different forms of intelligence.

Veterinarians tell remarkable stories. If we didn't know the lead character was an animal, we would be talking about awarding medals for valor. In one story, a cat rushed into a burning home, not once but six times, to save her kittens. In another, a ferret pulled a frightened kitten out of a deep hole. A cat in a nursing home always showed up to curl at the feet of a resident shortly before death offering comfort and companionship.

Family members remark upon how a dog that used to jump onto everyone's lap, now quietly inches his way up the bed. He seems to know that grandpa is very ill and lays his head near the old man's hand. Then there are the stories of the dog or cat that awoke a family from a burning house or steered a child away from danger. In another televised case a female gorilla gently moves a small child that has fallen into a gorilla exhibit away from the other gorillas to an area where zookeepers can reach the child.

Do you see your own virtues, personalities, and weaknesses in your animals? Have you learned more about who you really are? The stories you tell about your pets often reveal things about you. We have a pet story that has been retold countless times and even appeared in my former employer's newspaper. It was while reading Professor Tuan's remarks that a new insight came to me about why so many people enjoyed the story.

It was 5:00 AM on a dark, November, Saturday morning. Bob was out of town, and I was enjoying a sound, pleasant sleep, when all of a sudden, I heard our dogs,

Athena and Tasha, growling a "something seriously wrong is going on around here" growl. They'd jump on my bed, then jump off, run to the other room, and then come back to get me again. They were clearly trying to communicate.

I followed them into the guest bedroom where they were standing guard at the window. Looking out the second story window into the faint early morning light, I saw a male figure raising a ladder against the side of the house.

I called 911 and returned to the window. The dogs were pacing and emitting low guttural growls rather than barking loudly in their normal way. The ladder now was leaning on its side at the stranger's feet. He was standing with arms akimbo looking up in my direction. The curtains and darkness concealed me. Where are the police? I thought with a second of panic; then reason took over.

This looked like a teenager, not an adult. That gave me a little more sense of safety. Why would someone try to break into the second story of the house rather than the first floor? This was very odd.

I went downstairs to get a better look. With my faithful companions at my side, I had more confidence. I peeked out the sunroom windows that allowed me to see the entire backyard. He shrunk more; his big down jacket had made him seem larger. He turned toward the gate.

Adrenaline shot through me. He wasn't going to get away. I dashed to the kitchen door, threw on the yard light, let the dogs out, and yelled, "Stop right there! What do you think you are doing?" Athena and Tasha were only about fourteen pounds each, but that didn't stop them. They surrounded him and let loose a ruckus of barks and growls. He froze.

Just at that moment, two police officers came around the south side of the house fully prepared for trouble, hands close to their guns. They yelled something at him. Everyone froze. I called the dogs. They came immediately and stood beside me panting.

That broke the freeze tag. The police moved toward the boy and caught him by the arm. The boy's mouth began to work again, and he said something inane like, "It was the cat. I was just after my cat." He babbled more I couldn't hear. I joined the small circle.

It seemed the paper carrier had been delivering his route, when he heard a cat meowing. His missing cat was on my roof. He had seen the ladder behind our garage and thought he could reach the cat if he got up on the flat roof. However, he discovered that he wasn't strong enough to lift it against the house without possibly hitting a window. The police admonished him. "What if this lady had owned a gun?" was just one of the scenarios they painted for him.

Eventually, I fell asleep again until Bob called at 9:00 AM and teased me about sleeping in while he was gone. "You would, too, if you had been up half the night with a cat burglar," I replied. That certainly got his attention. Athena and Tasha became heroines. Although there wasn't any danger, it was great to know that my dogs recognized trouble and would act on it. Maybe they were reflecting a virtue that we humans value.

Stories Others Tell

We can be influenced by stories that others tell us about house and home. Think about the contrasts between the following storytellers.

Victor is Hispanic. He was born in a two-room house in a small town in Colorado. He became a teacher and has lived most of his adult life in Minnesota. He says that his family was quite poor, but his culture is rich with oral stories. They had no television but occasionally listened to the radio. The main form of entertainment and education was storytelling. His grandmother came often to stay, or they went to visit her. She was the matriarch of the family and the keeper of stories.

When work was done and dinner put away, the evening would begin. They would sit around a quiet room with an oil lamp. He remembers her house. It had a cloth ceiling, and a light breeze seemed to move it gently in time with the story. She told stories about everyone in the family including ancestors going back to the 1800s. The stories were endless, rich in variety, wisdom, and laughter. They were never bored.

At other times it was a mystical experience as the stories were related to religion and stories from the Bible. The rosary was said every night; it didn't matter if you were at home or in the truck. The mysteries of the rosary also told stories: the Joyful Mysteries, Sorrowful Mysteries, and the Glorious Mysteries.

Victor and his father spent a lot of time riding their horses for work and pleasure. There were stories then as well. There was also a great deal of profound silence as they experienced things together that did not need words.

I wonder if the most far-reaching storytellers in American culture have become the advertisers and the media, especially television and movies. If we watch a show on a makeover of a house, we are asking to receive ideas so that we are at least semi-conscious that what we are hearing or seeing is designed to influence us. Some companies have wonderful products and services. They need to advertise so that we can become aware of helpful items. We just need to be alert and teach our children the skill of being awake and filtering of information.

Commercials tell us stories, albeit much shorter ones. Again, they use visuals, characters, and music to offer promises too wonderful to resist. One story line is told over and over that originated in fairy tales. If we just buy the magic potion, we will achieve all our dreams. We seldom actively choose to watch a commercial; they are inflicted on us as a cost of watching something we did choose to see.

It is the subtle messages that creep into our psyches when we aren't asking to be influenced that can muffle our true desires or actually replace them with something artificial that isn't really us. On the other hand, they might teach us something worth remembering. The role of films is particularly interesting. Movies can catch us unawares both in a positive and negative sense.

Films have enormous emotional impact between the story, music, art, and graphics. If a film about an auto chase can make my stomach actually lurch, what can it do to my unconscious? I had a thoughtful and reflective conversation with Professor Hafed Bouassida,

Department Coordinator of the Cinema Division at Minneapolis Community and Technical College.

We discussed the two extremes of home messages. On the one hand there was the movie of *ET*, in which home is about belonging and the intense desire to "go home" again when we are separated from that home. In some ways it echoed a much earlier movie, *The Wizard of Oz*. In *ET*, home means a big home—your planet. Even the love of new friends and wondrous technology or beauty can't make up for our real home.

A more recent movie, *Avatar,* also raises issues about values and falling in love with a new home. This time, earthling Jake Sully falls in love with the beauty and wonder of the planet Pandora, as well as the indigenous peoples, their way of life, and Neytiri, the daughter of the clan's spiritual leader. As Jake comes to truly know himself, he is ready to die for this new home that has captured his spirit and heart. Somewhat like *Dances With Wolves,* this movie asks questions about our culture.

On the other end of the spectrum, Bouassida, talked about *The Truman Show*. He pointed out that the film really is a critique of how home had been reduced to nothing but a show. The show's host and its advertisers construct Truman's house, wife, friends, and his entire environment and also his inner reality of his beliefs and values. Even when Truman is pouring his heart out to his wife in a state of great agitation, she is trying to do a commercial. Bouassida said the film demonstrates that, "House and home have become what advertisers want it to be. They have stolen home from us."

Other movies come to mind. In the *Father of the Bride,* Parts I and II, George Banks struggles with house, home, and excessive wedding and remodeling costs. At moments he is touching as he recalls all the love and memories of the home he has just sold and moves mountains to get his home back. At other times he is made to look cheap when he validly challenges some of the costs of the perfect wedding and the baby's suite. The decorators produce a stunning event and addition to the house, but they have not enhanced the home.

In the movie, *Up,* we see a very different picture of home. In a span of a less than fifteen minutes, we see the fifty plus years of life of a loving couple—Carl and Ellie—from the time they meet until after Ellie's death. Photos, chairs, tables, are treasured items that are not to be moved. In those few moments we see life at peak moments of happiness and sadness and are moved by the beauty of relationships. As the story unfolds, 78-year-old Carl awakens to the grumpy, depressed person he has become since Ellie's death and sets out to reclaim the adventurers he and Ellie had been and meant to continue to be.

He loves his home and ties it to thousands of balloons meant to whisk him away to a spot in South America that had been part of his and Ellie's lost dream. To his shock and dismay, he learns he isn't alone on his journey, since Russell, an eight-year-old Boy Scout is on board. It is in the chaos of the relationship with Russell and two critters that also join the journey that Carl discovers where his heart really lies.

In *It's A Wonderful Life*, George Bailey struggles with the tug of his own dreams versus contributing to his community by staying in his hometown and running the Building and Loan. When crisis comes, he cannot bring himself to leave. He confronts Mr. Potter, the town banker, whose only love is money. George defends his father for starting the business and argues about the importance of people having their own homes.

He says, "He didn't save enough money to send Harry to school, let alone me. But he did help a few people get out of your slums, Mr. Potter, and what's wrong with that? Why—here, you're all businessmen here. Doesn't it make them better citizens? Doesn't it make them better customers? . . . Well, is it too much to have them work and pay and live and die in a couple of decent rooms and a bath? Anyway, my father didn't think so. People were human beings to him. But to you, a warped, frustrated old man, they're cattle. Well, in my book he died a much richer man than you'll ever be."

~

Reflections/Suggestions for Another Day:

• What stories are infused in your home?

• What kinds of stories do you tell? Are they action-oriented outer stories or stories that reveal your inner life as well?

• What is the role of stories in your family, friendships, and workplace?

• What stories do you tell yourself about your life?

- Who do you tell yourself you are? Who do others tell you that you are?
- What happens when you tell stories? Orally? Visually?
- What photographic stories are on display in your home? Who is their audience?
- What opportunities are waiting for you or those you love, if you created new inner stories?
- Do you have critter stories that tell you something about what you admire?
- What have you learned from movies or commercials that influences your perceptions about home?

Tested by Values

A list of important values could be long and drawn from many sources. We have our religious traditions and the insights learned from family and living. I have suggested that love is at the heart of every home and encompasses all those in the home and the home itself. Beyond love, you alone can decide on the values that are most important in your home. It is helpful to stop and ask, "What are our values and are we applying those in our most intimate lives?" This helps us to put our spirituality into daily living.

If we look at our common societal roots, there is food for thought. Socrates is still remembered 2500 years after his birth because he had a profound impact on philosophy and Western life. Yet, he never wrote a book. He had no power. He conquered no one. He never proclaimed he was wise or had answers. If he invented anything, it was the power of questions in the Socratic method. What he modeled was the examined life of someone who loved wisdom and sought to understand it.

If we were to follow his example, then part of our journey would be to not only define what we think it is to be just, good, or loving, but we would also want to listen to others to understand how they saw it. We would not tell others that our answers are the only right ones; we would ask questions seeking to understand a fuller picture. And we would do it connected to every day life, not just lofty thoughts.

Know thyself is a first step in the examined life. Home is the place we first become ourselves and are challenged to practice those values that we proclaim are important to us. It is also one of two places, the other being work, where we put theory into practice. What does it really mean to be honest, compassionate, generous, or just? These were the questions that Socrates asked. His prayer in the *Phaedrus* was, "May the outward and inward man be at one." In other words, may I know my inner self and may it be consistent with my outer self so that I am one integrated being.

We find another concept, both in Chinese history and in the works of Aristotle, called the Golden Mean and its related maxim, Nothing in Excess. This concept has particular relevance for homes in any society that has achieved some degree of abundance. You find the virtues and your center by living in the tension between extremes, avoiding excesses and deficiencies on any continuum. So the virtue of courage lies midway between recklessness, an excess and cowardice, a deficiency. This midpoint brings happiness and provides insight on the good life.

If you believe in "love thy neighbor" or the Golden Rule to treat others as you would like to be treated, then our homes challenge us to live those values with our neighbors. If we volunteer at church or donate to causes around the world, but don't care for our neighbors, Socrates would repeat his prayer that the outer and inner may be one. Perhaps someone on your street needs a ride to get groceries or a shoulder to lean on or a touch of forgiveness.

Do You Love Me?

What values are at the core of your home? How have your choices reflected your values? The natural process of all cultures is to create an unconscious picture of the right way to live. It is modeled to us from the time we are born by those around us, by our religious institutions, the media, and our schools. A common message is that once you are born, you are to grow, become educated, get a job, get married and have children, work hard, save money, enjoy yourself, decline with age, and die. Hopefully, along the way, we are encouraged to live a decent life—don't break the law, live ethically. In other words, we are handed recipes for life from a number of sources, and this is helpful.

Still, it isn't the whole picture because we do have choices. There is a risk for each of us that we will not live our life, but the life of the crowd. Life can be so full that a person can be carried along as if on autopilot. Well-intentioned people try to encourage us into certain careers and lifestyles. By even considering the differences between a house and a home, you have started down the path of the examined life.

There are two starting points for defining values. One is to ask what you believe are your values. The second starting point is to notice how you spend your life using time as the measure. Money is a secondary measure because we invested our time to acquire money. In the first approach we conceptually state our values. In the second, we look at behavior. The second is a more accurate measure of what we are doing, while the first may be what we aspire to do.

Once you have decided on those values, then the test is to continually examine if you are living those values. I say I love my home, but I notice how my home tests my love in a practical way when it comes to maintenance. It's the constant daily upkeep as well as the major repairs that can try the relationship. Maintenance feels boring, repetitive, or challenging. Who wants to clean the bathroom for the three hundredth time? Replacing a roof, water heater, or getting the toilet fixed just doesn't have that zing. I wondered if there was a way to embrace maintenance. If that is part of love, then I wanted to live that more fully.

I talked to our carpenter, Skip, and described my malaise. With a twinkle in his eye he said, "I know what you mean. I feel like that about my own house. My wife complains that everyone else's house gets fixed before ours." He stopped and laughed as though recalling conversations.

"She's right, of course. It's more fun to build an

addition to someone else's house than to fix a sticking door on ours. I finally decided that my house is like a living entity or a family member. It needs attention just like my body needs daily food and rest or like my kids need daily attention. Your house isn't inert material. It is alive and growing or decaying."

"A living entity or family member," that really struck me. My home was a friend, but I thought of it that way when I was beautifying and enjoying it, a major improvement felt similar to falling in love. Somehow, when my home demanded something of me, it was easier to forget that. We do the same thing in human relationships, so it isn't surprising that we do it to our homes.

Perhaps I could respond out of gratitude rather than begrudgingly. I smiled to myself, remembering an ad I had heard on the radio. In it, the furnace had a voice and woke the owners up at night about needing servicing. From then on I tried to deal with these external repairs by changing my internal perception of them.

Gratitude is a powerful place from which to come. If the furnace needed to be repaired, gratitude for heat and warmth might thaw my icy response. Gratitude, like love, is boundless. If the sink was leaking, *I* could leak with appreciation. It could pour out of me and turn into the joy of having running water; many do not have that. I'm so thankful for showers. That is miraculous. Enough imagination could push that gratitude out into the sewer system and to a good city that manages it. Well, you can see what I mean.

Here is a second idea. One of the fun things about

beauty is sharing it with someone else. Maintenance is not something we tend to share with others. Why not? My friend, Tabitha, was coming over after we had replaced the furnace. I told her the saga of this issue. She was willing to admire my new furnace and the warmth that it was providing as well as its quiet running. One of her values is environmental stewardship, so her appreciation of the furnace's positive environmental rating was sincere. A furnace can be beautiful, too.

If gratitude could do all that with a home, imagine what it could do for human relationships. It's the daily upkeep of a relationship that can try our nerves. Loving is so easy when things are going smoothly, and no one is asking anything from us.

I'll Just Curl Up Here and Stay Awhile

No wonder we want a place where we can seek refuge, a place to relieve our thirst for meaning, a touch of joy and comfort, a place to renew. In the 2006 Stress & Anxiety Disorders Survey, half of Americans reported excessive stress from work that affected their work performance and home life. Over 80% reported that stress affected their relationships with their spouse or significant other, and a third said it also spilled over on their children. Even very young children are showing signs of unhealthy stress. No one values stress, so why do we have so much of it? Are we dealing with it in a way that is consistent with our values? The most common things people turn to for relief are sleep, food, friends, drugs, caffeine, smoking, exercise, and alcohol.

Gallop Research has conducted a global research project that is reported in the book, *The Five Essential Elements of Wellbeing.* The five are:

• Career Wellbeing—this relates to enjoying how you spend your time at work and besides at work

• Social Wellbeing—you need strong relationships in your life whether you are an introvert or extrovert

• Financial Wellbeing—managing your economic life wisely, regardless of income

• Physical Wellbeing—caring for your health and energy levels

• Community Wellbeing—your sense of engagement where you live

Perhaps the most startling data for me was that only 7% of us are thriving in all five areas. The authors point out that we are our worst enemies when we make short-term decisions that are not in our best interest. As you can see all of these relate to how we live at home. Even the career issue relates significantly to home because how we live at home determines a great deal of our financial needs which then allow us or restrain us from finding work that is meaningful in addition to lucrative.

So we should turn to our homes for help with all these issues. In a popular business management book of the '80s, *Megatrends,* author John Naisbitt cited one of the top ten trends affecting our lives as High Tech, High Touch. The focus wasn't on stress, but it was related to the feeling of being overwhelmed by industrialized jobs and the impersonalization of life.

Naisbitt had tracked how a parallel redeeming trend sought to balance this. The human potential movement tried to restore a sense of human scale and human touch to meet our emotional and spiritual needs. The more high tech in our lives, the more high touch we need to establish balance and a golden mean. That high touch response is still relevant and is found in your home. It is in the relationships, the beauty, creative acts, and meaningful stories. A loving and beautiful home can heal you.

I've had a profound experience with this. About eight months before our daughter's wedding, I experienced my first flare up of rheumatoid arthritis. It was severe and debilitating. My hands, shoulders, knees, and feet were so swollen and painful that I couldn't dress myself, drive, or do much of anything. I had always been pretty healthy, so this was a shock.

Over the years my clients had included a number of health organizations on holistic healthcare and Earl Bakken, the founder of Medtronic and inventor of the battery powered pacemaker. He, also, had helped develop a holistic hospital in Hawaii so I was very aware of complementary medicine and the importance of diet in healing. I put my consulting related knowledge to work on my own behalf.

I found a great rheumatologist and a wonderful naturopath with whom to work. My naturopath put me on an organic, anti-inflammatory, hypoallergenic diet, and some supplements. That means lots of fruits and vegetables, certain grains and legumes, and no red meats. My rheumatologist was skeptical but willing to monitor me if I wanted to try that approach first.

My family surrounded me in love and help, as did my home. At first I felt very lonely since I couldn't leave the house, but all the years of creating a home turned out to contribute to a very healing place that was instrumental in my emotional and spiritual health, which, in turn, helped improve my physical health. Two friends who are former home-economics teachers, Mary and Anne, came and helped me adjust to the new diet—both teaching me and actually preparing meals. I also did four hours a day of hand therapy exercises.

My rheumatologist was surprised, but supportive, as he documented my slow but continuous improvement. He said, "There aren't studies that prove that this diet works, but I can't deny what my eyes are showing me and what your blood work report tells me; you clearly are improving." I did end up needing some medications as well, but I am confident that the whole combination has helped me return to normal and avoid the negative side effects of the drugs.

Places are powerful. Winston Churchill described this when he said, "We shape our buildings; thereafter, they shape us." When we create our oasis, we want to stay there and not always go running off. It can help us stay well and return to health if we work with our homes as partners. How can it replenish us, if we are in and out? It also would be helpful to our health and well-being if our homes ran on a different cultural clock than work—one that is slower and paced around love.

Edie has much insight on diverse cultures. She was born in Germany and moved to Minnesota after her marriage to an American. She taught German and then started a non-profit with her husband. It focuses on working with language teachers to provide high school students with language immersion programs and travel in other countries. I chaired the Board of Directors for several years. She has traveled extensively. We talked about cultural time, beginning, of course, with German time.

Time in Germany is even more extremely punctual than in the United States, she explained. There are a number of factors that encourage that. One is that Germans rely heavily on public transportation. The train or bus is not forgiving if you are late. Secondly, people shop for fruits, vegetables, bread, and meat daily except for weekends. The store hours are shorter than in the United States, so you have to get from work to the store and home in a regimented way. The stores also have few weekend hours. The larger message is that people are not alive to consume but to rest and relax with family.

Then she talked about Spanish cultures. She now lives part of the year in Mexico. She has adjusted to a very different clock. Time doesn't really matter. Things begin when people get there. Agreeing that someone will come over at 9:00 AM doesn't really mean too much. Showing up unannounced is not seen as inappropriate because if we are friends and family, people come first and you adapt to their needs. You definitely don't interrupt a conversation to go rushing off. It is a very different world than Germany or the United States.

If we want the good life, we need to establish our own Golden Mean around balance. What we balance can vary from person to person and family to family. Achieving balance would be of benefit to all. The greatest balance is between engaging in the outer world and relaxing and reflecting into our inner world. It is almost as if the day and the seasons were designed to signal this need. Day calls us outside; night calls us inside. Spring and summer are the responsorial verses to fall and winter.

Modern life begs us to ask a new more complex question beyond balance. It's the questions that you ask that lead you into a new creative space. If you keep asking the same question and get the same answer or an insufficient answer, it's time for a new question. It also may be time for a vision. Home allows you to practice big issues in small, practical, and tangible ways. The new question is, "How do we integrate our lives and values so that one action solves multiple desires?" Having dinner together is one of those opportunities.

Dinner, Anyone?

We love our families; yet, one of our biggest challenges is making time to share a daily meal. It, along with story telling, is one of the most ancient social activities on earth as discussed earlier about the power of storytelling. Today, it is a ritual that is harder and harder to achieve. Even for those who are single, it can be hard to make a healthy meal and eat it at leisure.

Our homes and families ask us to overcome all the barriers. The changes in working trends contribute to this. More and more households have dual working adults, more senior citizens are working, and many young people have part-time jobs. In Juliet Schor's book, *The Over-worked American,* she documents a number of trends that suggest that individually and collectively, Americans have created a way of life that requires more work and less leisure time to be home:

• The average American owns and consumes two to three times more than 20–30 years ago but has less free time.

• Americans spend more time shopping than any other country and spend a higher fraction of what they earn.

• The majority of people work an extra month per year compared to the past. Ironically, while nearly a fifth of Americans are unable to secure a full-time job that meets their needs, the rest are working too hard. So we have the over-employed, underemployed, and unemployed but lack the Golden Mean of the balanced employed.

• Despite a significant increase in labor saving devices in the home, new expectations about house work mean that women (and some men) have not gained any leisure time.

• Parental time with children has fallen about ten hours per week for white parents and twelve hours per week for black parents.

For homes with children, the wealth of participation activities available and the huge chunks of time and chauffeuring required add a second significant road-block. It's challenging to have a half hour a day to relax together. A group of parents in a Minneapolis suburb successfully rallied together to demand changes from the school and athletic associations concerning the amount and times of practices and games. Other parents limit the number of activities allowed.

They did it because they know the truth and weren't willing to give up. Dining together can be one of the greatest binding rituals we can perform. The critical part—no television or other electronic device is invited to dinner. If you are dining together, you are fully present to each other wanting to share. Eating together might mean everyone is at the table, but focused on the television, or that rather than sharing, they are tearing at each other.

What we eat matters as we are setting ourselves up for more health or more illness. I have come to believe that how food is grown also matters. The first book I read

about this was in the mid-1970s. Paul Hawken wrote a book, *The Magic of Findhorn*. He describes a small community in northern Scotland called Findhorn where people grow forty-pound cabbages and huge flowers, plants and vegetables of all types on soil that by all rights shouldn't be able to grow much of anything. Being a skeptic, he decided to visit this place. He found a spiritual community and a worldview that believed in and acted on connectivity. It showed up in tangible ways in the food they produced and ate.

Studies document the benefits that can be attained by regular family meals: increased communication, superior academic performance, better nutrition, and healthier emotional well-being. Nancy Gibbs writes in a *Time* magazine article titled, "The Magic of the Family Meal," that it isn't just young children who benefit.

"It's in the teenage years that this daily investment pays some of its biggest dividends. Studies show that the more often families eat together, the less likely kids are to smoke, drink, do drugs, get depressed, develop eating disorders, and consider suicide, and the more likely they are to do well in school, delay having sex, eat their vegetables, learn big words, and know which fork to use."

If you eat alone, it also matters how you do it, you could have music to relax or inspire you or perhaps you share dinner with your pet or your home as a companion. This is an area in which electronics can have a positive role if they are used to bring people together. Karen is a single mom whose kids are grown and away at college or work. Once a week, she has dinner with her daughter via the speakerphone settings on their cell phones. Another night, she puts a tray on her lap and sits by the computer because her son prefers visual contact, as well as auditory, so they spend time together via iChat or Skype.

How would you like to have two months a year of leisure time, for not only dinner, but also anything else that you enjoy? According to the A.C. Nielsen Co., the average American watches more than four hours of TV each day or twenty-eight hours per week, or two months of nonstop TV-watching per year. In a sixty-five year life, that person will have spent almost eleven years glued to the tube. And 66% of us regularly watch television during dinner. Yes, employers, schools, athletics, and other activities pose a challenge, but it appears from these statistics that we do have a choice.

If you are struggling with this issue, congratulations. You have taken on the beast and are stepping forward. It will take warrior energy to win this one. Protecting that precious time may demand you pick up a strong shield and a sharp sword to pierce through to the heart of what matters and rescue it. At the journey's end, you will be a hero. You may even have saved a life.

Suggestion #1—Find your own reasons for doing this; guilt isn't particularly helpful. Create a vision.

Suggestion #2—Take the long and wide view. What are your most important values about the future that are affected by this struggle? What are the risks and rewards of the alternatives as you see them?

Suggestion #3—If you can't carve out the mealtime, explore if there is another block of time to talk with those who matter.

Suggestion #4—Someone has already found a path. Get support from them.

Define: "Enough"

If you can define "enough" for yourself and your home, you may simultaneously define happiness. A renewed interest in "Nothing in Excess" could bring us more happiness as well. A visual image of your answers could be captured in a balanced scale. Is it balanced or weighted too much in one direction?

This just might be the most significant issue facing the United States. Are we overeating? Over spending? Over our heads in debt? Over working? Over powering? Overly concerned about getting ahead or making more money? If we are overdoing something in one part of our lives, then we are suffering in another area.

There is a new movement afoot in architecture, as well, that asks these questions. It was launched by Sarah Susanka's book, *The Not So Big House*. She says, "There is a deep yearning for something more. The paradox is that something more resides in less. More quality, less quantity. More beauty, less bravado. More inner abundance, less outer display of wealth . . . this move to do more with less arises from a generosity of spirit: a wish for sufficiency instead of overindulgence." Her message seems to be taking hold. New home median sizes shrank in both 2008 and 2009. We have a way to go compared to other countries. In 2007, the average American home was about

2500 square feet; in the same time period, the average house in Germany and France was 1200 square feet and 900 square feet in England.

It is at home that you most confront your values about what matters in life because home is where you are the decision-maker. It is where you put your values into every day practice or discover that the price of something you say you value is higher than what you are willing to pay. This includes both tangible things and intangibles such as how much time we give to whom and to what.

A walk through your home and activities will tell you the truth about who you are in practice, as opposed to in principle. It may raise some questions, just like a good friend. If I say I am a generous person, but my tax files show insignificant contributions, and my appointment book shows no volunteer work, my home is asking, "Who did you say you were?" If I see myself as lacking in artistic skills, but my garden is beautiful and my meals mouthwatering, my home may suggest, "Look here, see, you are an artist. You value creativity."

Looking at your "stuff," will tell you a great deal. First, you might want to look at the sheer quantity of what you own. One of the biggest new product areas in the last ten years is designed to provide storage and organization systems. It includes closet systems, cabinets, plastic storage boxes, sheds, and rental units for storage.

Akiko Busch, author of *Geography of Home,* comments on the growing volume of storage: "The idea behind these myriad storage units is that they are going to help you organize your life, simplify it even. Common sense might dictate that if it is simplification you're after, buying less might be a more direct route. But the message such catalogs put out is that you can possess forty pairs of shoes and still live simply, just so long as you're also outfitted with the multi-tiered cabinet in which to neatly stack them."

Having things organized is a many-flavored advantage, if what you have is good for you and for others. Busch's point is to ask what it is you really want and go directly after that, rather than be caught in a charade. Is it simplicity you desire or organization? Is it the shoes you want, or is there something the shoes represent that calls to you?

Janelle had stuff everywhere. There was little room for anything else, even her body. Getting from the kitchen through the dining room to the living room was a treacherous journey; there were too many things that could accidently be bumped, causing something to break, or a stack of items to end up on the floor blocking forward movement. Cabinet and closets were stacked high with boxes, the basement was full, the garage had no room for the car, the garden shed was overflowing, and her monthly rental cost for a storage facility annoyed her. She joked that her only remaining recourse was to buy a bigger house.

She wanted a change but needed an additional impetus to motivate her to act on her dissatisfaction. Despite the living room, the majority of her things were organized so that wasn't the major issue. She asked friends for ideas. Three comments resonated with her.

One friend merely shared a quote. "Get rid of anything that isn't useful, beautiful, or joyful." Another person said, "Your essence is generosity; try focusing on how much you could give others who need your things much more than you do." The third asked her if she had ever added up the total cost of storing everything she had. When she did that, she was shocked. The combination of the three ideas helped her find a path to defining her answer to the question, "What is enough?" For her it included a new budget goal for storage costs, a motivation for giving things away, and a sorting process for what to keep or give away.

Exercise—Total Costs of Storage

• Estimate the costs of storage containers you currently have or what you would need from things as small as a plastic box to things as large as a shed.

• Determine what percentage of your monthly mortgage and property taxes are for the garage and convert that into a dollar amount.

• Add the square footage of your home that is used for storage including cabinets, cupboards, and closets. Storage for holiday items, off season clothes, and equipment are also part of this category.

• Determine what percentage of the total house your storage square footage is and translate that into a dollar figure given your mortgage and property taxes.

• Determine what the costs are for insurance or security systems for your storage areas.

• Add all of these costs, except for the storage containers, to get your monthly storage costs.

• Examine how you feel about those costs.

Money, Money, Money

What we really want in life is a home that provides us with happiness, health, and love. Yet, we seem to get caught up in money issues, no matter what we want and which way we turn. This is an area in which, if we want happiness to win out, then we need to be very tough and honest with ourselves. If you can find some quotes or statistics that drive home for you the points you most need to remember, they can act like a North Star for you. The following are a few of mine:

"We are not human beings having a spiritual experience. We are spiritual beings having a human experience," wrote Teilhard De Chardin. This reminds me of my true identity and purpose.

"Most people have work that is too small for their spirits," revealed Studs Terkel. Like the quote above, this challenges me to do work that is large enough for my spirit.

"The cost of a thing is the amount of what I call life which is required to be exchanged for it, immediately or in the long run." Henry David Thoreau's words certainly give me perspective when tempted to buy things since I am trading part of my life for them.

"Are you making a living or making a dying by the way you work and the way you manage money?" The authors of *Your Money or Your Life* ask bluntly. This applies not just to me, but also to how I work with my loved ones and my clients.

Many years ago I attended a workshop on money. The facilitator asked the question, "What are your earliest childhood memories about money?" The answers we all gave were diverse. Some had learned that money was for doing good deeds. Others had learned that money was a measure of one's worth as a human being. Still others had learned that they and their families weren't worth much.

An additional lesson that arose out of our discussion was that these money lessons had a great deal of emotional power that we don't see on a daily basis. That power can drive us the wrong way. The next question I explored was, "What did those memories teach me and are those lessons serving me or destroying me?"

Bill's problem was his monthly stack of bills. His fiancé, Sheryl, could see he was on a troublesome path that would end up becoming hers. His love of sporting equipment and the newest electronic devices were his two biggest weaknesses. In addition, he was carrying school debt. The marriage preparation process through church provided Sheryl with a mechanism to start a conversation that was uncomfortable.

It opened the door, but Sheryl didn't feel that the conversation was going to lead to change. She waited a while, hoping she was wrong. After seeing Bill's newest unnecessary purchase, she was upset. She confided in Jan, her older married sister.

Jan also saw a big problem and shared what some of her experiences had been. She encouraged Sheryl to solve this before they got married. She suggested trying a mindset as to how Bill and Sheryl would want to live in the future, rather than labeling Bill as the problem. They could create some goals together such as buying a house.

Then they should share what their current financial situation was and agree on a new budget. They could also try to eliminate debt before they were married or agree on who was responsible for existing debt.

Sheryl felt those were helpful ideas. Then she did not feel as though she was criticizing Bill. They would be a team looking at the present and future. That made her more confident in approaching Bill. He was responsive to Sheryl's approach, but they also had a surprise. In the course of the conversation, his emotional need to buy all this stuff surfaced. As they discussed that, Bill said that ever since he was a young child, his family had labeled him as the "technology-whiz-kid." He wore that title like a badge of honor as a child, so he had to be up on everything. The twenty-six-year-old Bill didn't really need that any more.

Another way to define "enough" and to stay focused on happiness is to establish a money strategy that reflects your shared values. When we were young and about to get married, we knew our different family financial backgrounds had made some permanent impressions in our approach to budgets and spending. We could see conflicts ahead. We agreed to a money strategy. It had six components that answered our big questions. What was our money philosophy and goals? What is enough for the family? Contributions? Savings? Individual spending?

1) We agreed that our philosophy was to live within our means to a large degree and to maintain the financial freedom to change jobs or careers if need be. That included all the categories just mentioned. There was an appropriate time for debt and credit card usage, but it

was quite limited. We would have to get loans for large purchases like a house or cars, but our goals were to pay those off early and live debt free most of our lives. Maintaining a comfortable and modest daily lifestyle was the key to achieving this. For us, credit cards were a convenience tool, not a cash source. So, if we used them, the expectation was that we would be able to pay them off in 30–60 days. When debit cards appeared, we switched to them to a large degree.

2) We agreed on a monthly household budget including food, utilities, rent/mortgage, family gifts, and entertainment. We also agreed on donations and savings. We set up one checking account for those items.

3) We set up savings and investment accounts and worked with some financial advisors. The joint household account would feed into these. Any extra money beyond paychecks such as bonuses, overtime, and gifts also fed into this.

4) We proportioned the expenses between us based on income level. When we received our paychecks, we had to pay the household account first. There were no exceptions.

5) Then we each had our own checking accounts that covered our car payments, haircuts, clothing, lunch expenses, and anything else that was personal choice including additional savings. The only limitation on our own spending was that we not exceed our individual ability to pay. We did not have any joint credit cards. So if one of us bought something the other person thought was frivolous, it didn't matter as long as we had stuck to the agreements.

6) When we had a child, all of the basic expenses became part of the household budget. Extra fun things were part of our individual discretionary accounts.

This worked for us. It acknowledged that we were a family and had responsibilities first to the family. Yet, it also gave some freedom and accountability to us as individuals. It eliminated many arguments. You could adapt this to your own situation. If you do not have enough income for this approach, you could still give yourselves a small allowance for personal decisions. If you have one income, be honest; the other person is contributing to the household in other ways, so put a dollar value on it and deal with it fairly. Various economists have tried to estimate this with different approaches that you can find on the Internet.

There are three books that take different approaches to the questions of beliefs, values, and money that you might find intriguing. See the appendix for *Your Money or Your Life, Think and Grow Rich,* and *Money Is My Friend.* They are quite different, which is helpful to exploring your values.

The first book has many useful exercises for understanding your relationship to money: what is enough, setting budgets and dreams, and achieving a different kind of financial independence from a values-based perspective. The second book has been around since 1937 and explores the relationship between your beliefs and growing rich and a series of steps for the action-oriented. It is the inner process of beliefs that most interested me. The third one addresses some of the same issues and more but from the perspective of the laws of money. It is a different kind of read for the more analytical. Elements of the three combined make an interesting whole since you see the same issues through different eyes.

Buying Considerations

Our society shops as a form of entertainment or a national sport. At times that leads us to buy things we would have been happy without. At other times we come home delighted that we have found exactly what we wanted. For a significant percentage of U.S. homes, shopping is changing.

More people are asking new questions. Will this carpet emit unhealthy emissions into my home? Was this made with sweatshop labor? Is this biodegradable? Should I use plastic or paper bags? Is this locally produced and organically grown?

Change can be hard, but it doesn't have to be. In hindsight, I find it perplexing that learning to carry cloth bags for shopping, rather than accepting plastic or paper bags took as long as it did. Change can be fun.

I've learned that bamboo is an incredible plant. I heard about it at a Parade of Homes show from my favorite architectural firm, SALA Architects, in a discussion about flooring. Since I wasn't putting in floors, it was interesting, but it didn't seem relevant to me at the time. When I learned that it is also used in fabrics, suddenly that information about bamboo lodged some place in my brain perked up.

It was a fun discovery process and interesting. I learned

that sheets, clothing, and gardening gloves, to name a few, could be made of bamboo. I was a little skeptical that I wanted it near my skin. It sounded hard and scratchy. The only way to know was to try it. I tried garden gloves first and loved them. They feel like silk, yet are strong and more flexible than my other gloves. They dry twice as fast as cotton. The squirrels like them, too. After a glove disappeared, I thought I saw something up in a tree. After the next windy day, I found my glove on the ground. I don't leave them outside any more.

Now my favorite sheets are made of bamboo; they seem softer and more temperature perfect than any sheets I've ever had. I also have a simple, elegant tunic. It can be dressed up or down. Bamboo can also be spun into yarn.

Environmental facts about bamboo plants:

• Bamboo plants can grow successfully without any fertilizers or pesticides.

• Bamboo grows extremely fast—it's the fastest growing plant on the planet. It has been known to grow 3–4 feet per day.

• Bamboo doesn't require a lot of water to grow.

• Bamboo is a hardy plant—it can survive drought conditions and flood conditions.

• Bamboo plants release oxygen into the air. A grove of bamboo releases 35% more oxygen than an equivalent stand of trees.

• Bamboo is an earth friendly plant. It can reduce soil erosion and desertization. It can actually improve soil quality in degraded and eroded areas.

We can also ask new questions before we start buying. If you want to save money, or the environment, or both, and want to freshen up your home or wardrobe, an excellent new rule of thumb before shopping could help you. Stop and ask yourself, "What level of escalation is called for?" And "What would be creative?" When you have a backache, you wouldn't jump to surgery as your first action, so too with buying.

First, consider whether a simple small action could make a big difference. Level one interventions involve moving things—pillows, curtains, or other accessories—within the room or from one room to another—a vase, a chair, or a small table. We explored this earlier in "Moving Beauty." You can swap any of these things with a friend who is also in the doldrums and move things from one home to another.

If that doesn't work, then escalate to level two—transforming your walls. Consider painting, wallpapering, or any other form of artistic endeavor. Maybe you just need to change one wall. Paint one wall a different color, or wallpaper it to complement the rest of the room. Add detail or color contrast to a cabinet, wall, or door like the stories of my linen closet and fireplace. Do a small stencil in a special area. Details have a great impact.

Still not enough? Then onward to level three—Buy a grouping of small things like pillows and throws that brighten the room or one big thing that will have a major impact. A large interesting plant can change a room. Perhaps it is a new rug or piece of furniture. Make it something special by connecting it to an anniversary or birthday. It could be the 10th anniversary of moving into your home.

The next step, level four is to do a small intervention that has a real kick. Have something built to change a room or remove a wall or cabinets like the example of my kitchen cabinets. Having it custom made by you or someone you know can have meaning as well as function.

The last option is level five. Do a major intervention that creates a whole new room. For some people, it may be an addition. Leverage this to the max, not in terms of money spent, but in value received. Try for an abundance of desires being met in the one action. Seek beauty in the room, but think about what other desires you have that could be part of the same experience. Perhaps it is an opportunity to deepen your relationships, involve the whole family in an activity. Be creative and learn something new.

Valuing Advice

All of these issues of home, family, dinner, enoughness, and responsible-buying are related to the ethics of home. Home is a place for living out our values and ethics, for teaching them, and for receiving advice about them. Many of us turn to our religious leaders and advisors for answers to questions of values. Others turn to philosophers.

Philosopher Tom Morris offers insight about ethics in *If Aristotle Ran General Motors*. He says, "Ethics is all about spiritually healthy people in socially harmonious relationships." Ethics marries the inner development of the individual with the outer aspects of harmonious relationships. Making the connection between the individual and others is the hard part. So when you are choosing advisors, you might consider whether you can work in harmony in these two dimensions.

Morris goes on to say, "Social harmony is not only a state of the absence of conflict but one of positive, vibrant consonance and interpersonal strength, a relationship within which individuals can attain the development of their highest gifts and enjoy the fullness of life together. This is the concern of ethics. The harmony of guitar strings vibrating together produces what no particular string could give rise to alone."

Most of us do not have the time, talent, equipment, or legal certification to do everything relating to our homes that we would like to do. So we turn to plumbers, electricians, painters, carpenters, builders, interior designers, and a host of other people to assist us. We may also need attorneys, doctors, tax accountants, financial advisors, insurance agents, veterinarians, realtors, and other professionals. These experts help you with your important decisions.

Values are part of these relationships in one form or another, but they may be in the background of the conversations. In a meaningful home, they usually are in the center of the conversations. You want the relationship between you and your advisors to "vibrate together" as Morris says. There is the obvious value proposition as in, "What are you going to charge me, and what do we get in return?" That is important, but it is not what I want to explore with you.

Do those you hire as advisors share your vision and value system about home? If they don't share it, can they advise you well by honoring your values, even if they do not share them? You can trust someone's competency, but you may not trust his or her compatibility.

We began using a financial advisor long before we had much money to invest. We were looking for a long-term relationship based on competence, compatibility, and trust. Jill met all our criteria. By compatibility, we meant someone who shared our values and could advise from within that worldview, or who would listen closely to our view, respect it, and advise with that in mind.

At one point, a friend strongly recommended another financial advisor, Frank. Bob and I agreed that it might be wise to try an experiment. We had made a lot of progress toward paying off our mortgage early. We had both had a good year and knew we would have bonuses and profit sharing. If combined, that could bring us very close to paying off the mortgage. That had been a priority for a long time and was conveyed to both the current advisor and the new prospective advisor. We wanted, however, to have a thorough understanding of the ramifications of that decision. Should we pay off the mortgage or invest our bonuses?

We gave the same questions and information to both advisors. Each asked his or her specific questions, which were quite different. Jill recommended proceeding with our plan to pay off the house loan despite the loss of some tax advantages for the mortgage deduction. Frank was against paying off the mortgage, arguing that we needed the tax deduction. He also projected a larger financial loss than Jill had forecasted.

We circled back around to Jill with Frank's comments and then back to Frank. At the end of the process our conclusions were that Jill understood us better, had factored in more financial issues than the tax implications and was providing holistic advice. One of her unique questions had been, "If you didn't have the mortgage payment, what would you do with the money? Do you have other dreams that your home could support in addition to the freedom from the mortgage?" Her financial analysis had included those answers; that changed the numbers and provided a more authentic picture that went beyond dollars to value.

Jill got married and her spouse, Jim, joined the business. We found an even greater affinity because by now we were doing more investing. Jim was well versed in socially responsible investing and personally committed to that. That approach to investing was a good fit. I've been to workshops or heard radio financial investing interviews that have frustrated me. Audience members will express an interest in values and investing. The commentators totally ignore what the person has said and return to talking about maximizing wealth. My message isn't that you should invest in any particular way; the message is to use advisors who listen to your values.

Alecia, our interior designer, was a wonderful listener. Working with her was somewhat like having a dance partner. We were listening to the same music (values, desires, vision), but she often led and I followed. When I had an insight and wanted to lead, she could follow. She was a good teacher as well, discussing the principles under her recommendations. When I would step on her feet or call a halt, she was responsive and engaged.

I've also mention Skip, my house doctor. He cares about our house. He is like the good uncle, who remembers what some niece or nephew did at an earlier age and how that is now affecting the current reality. He has poked and prodded so many areas that when something new comes up, he can see how that is interconnected with other issues. He is trustworthy, honest, and versatile. He recommends others when he doesn't feel he should tackle some issue. Perhaps I could find someone more skilled at a particular thing, but I like the bigger picture that I get with him better.

~

Reflections/Suggestions for Another Day

• What values are primary in your home when you look at your behavior?

• What values do you aspire to if they are different than what your behavior is?

• How stressed are you and how does that affect your home?

• How much time would you need to stay home enough for your home to restore you?

• What is dinner hour like in your home?

• What are your definitions of "enough" in all the major areas of your home?

• How much values clarification do you do before spending money on your home?

• How much of your life are you spending to acquire money or things?

• How do you define happiness?

• Are your advisors a good values fit?

• Who and what are you really working for?

• What tradeoffs are you making relating to money?

• Are they bringing you lasting happiness?

• What effects are your decisions having on the happiness of others?

• How are you going to take the next step toward your dreams?

Fulfilled by Contribution

Many fields of study from philosophy to theology to political science debate what the true natural state of the human soul is. Are we born greedy or generous? Are we born with an orientation toward the good, or are we a blank slate? I suspect we are born wanting to live, to share, and to last. We want to be part of a community if for no other reason than this would be wise because we wouldn't survive without others.

When communities are smaller and closer to nature, it's easier to see our connections. Sharing a resource or space needed by all, makes us aware we have to be careful about our collective and individual use. Hunter and gatherer societies needed each other to find food. Farmers needed each other to help build barns, gather the harvest, and transport their goods. Roman law even recognized four kinds of property rights, one of which was *res communes,* common things accessible to all that can't be exclusively possessed by individuals or government like the pastures for animals or running water. *The Magna*

Carta, signed in England in 1215, established fisheries as a res communes. The Boston Commons was once a shared sheep pasture.

Peter Barnes is the author of *Who Owns the Sky?* He raises contemporary questions about this concept. He is exploring ancient ideas, like res communes, in new forms to try to solve global problems like the need for clean air—something that would benefit everyone on the planet. By asking, "Who owns the sky?" he is asking who is responsible for this common good, and how can we give everyone a stake in caring for it?

As societies become more complex and larger, our ability to see our interconnectedness diminishes. This seems counter intuitive because in other ways we know how much more linked we are. The Internet, television, and radio take us into the lives of people all over the world on a daily basis. Individuals can do good deeds, but it takes individuals working together as communities to do great work such as clean the air, build a cathedral, foster democracy, recover from a disaster, or help us to learn to care for the strangers down the block.

A house isn't all that interested in these things. Its concern is focused on if anything around it will make the house look better or increase in value. A home, on the other hand, wants to give because it feels right, it's empowering, and it's so satisfying to know you matter. The home wants an I-Thou relationship with its community in which there is caring, respect, and give and take.

Outside Matters

There are many aspects to homes—from your relationships in the home, to making your physical home a lovely and inviting place, to the stories and values that give meaning to the life of your home. There is yet another dimension to home that is worth exploration. That is the portion of home that extends beyond four walls. Those people and things that are outside of your house have a significant impact on your home and its inhabitants.

Houses are aware of this in one main dimension; if something affects property values, houses notice. A home, though, is very aware that it is a part of a much larger whole. It knows that it cannot sever its connection with its yard, streets, neighbors, and community without spilling its own life supply.

Yards, which some architects refer to as outside rooms, are an important part of home. Even a few minutes of sitting out in the yard can refresh every aspect of your being. If you're down, it can lift you up. If you're sick, you may feel better. If you're happy, you can be even happier. If you're worried, you may find a little peace. A whole day spent in your garden may leave you wonderfully aching, but your heart and soul will be singing.

Many little things can have such a big impact, you almost feel as if you have regained your child-like awe and wonder. A big fat worm that your child has found can make you smile. Sometimes, I am so thrilled about the hummingbird I just saw that I run into the house to get my camera, and then I sit quietly for long stretches hoping it will come back.

Watching two small birds carry straw and sticks into the birdhouse pleases me. Seeing some new buds on the first flowers of spring speaks volumes. Taking the time to watch spring plants grow is amazing. You can actually see them grow. Perhaps you fret over leaves of a red twigged dogwood that seems to have something eating at it. This fall I checked the Jackman Clematis in the front of the house every day. It was still blooming as temperatures dipped lower and lower, and every other flower in sight was long gone. Our yards allow a daily immersion in nature with all its benefits if we just stop to notice.

"Elderly adults tend to live longer if their homes are near a park or other green space, regardless of their social or economic status. College students do better on cognitive tests when their dorm windows view natural settings. Children with ADHD have fewer symptoms after outdoor activities in lush environments. Residents of public housing complexes report better family interactions when they live near trees. These are only a few of the findings from recent studies that support the idea that nature is essential to the physical, psychological, and social well-being of the human animal," said Frances Kuo, Professor of Natural Resources and Environmental Science and Psychology at the University of Illinois.

Humans suffer a variety of negative social effects when living in barren landscapes that lack greenery. Kuo and her colleagues have shown that these effects include decreased civility, less supervision of children outdoors, and more illegal activity, aggression, property crime, loitering, graffiti and litter. "We might call some of that 'soiling the nest,' which is not healthy," she said. "No organisms do that when they're in good shape."

Just as flowers have an impact on people in a room, our natural habit has an impact, not just on individuals, but also on the city. Considerable research has found that violence and aggression are highest in urban settings devoid of trees and grass. Other researchers have found that cities with access to nature positively influences moods, life attitudes, and work satisfaction.

A yard that is not cared for creates impressions about the home and the people inside of it. Your neighbors' yards also affect your home. If most of the neighborhood looks as if people do not care about their yards, graffiti, vandalism, and crime are more likely to take root and spread, like a noxious and invasive plant. If they are loved and tended, that caring is also likely to spread.

Joan lived in the city on a busy street with crime an ever-present reality. She read an article one day about the potential that gardens had for reducing crime and took the insight to heart. For Joan, who had grown up on a farm, gardens were already meaningful. Over the last years as she had recovered from cancer, a divorce, and subsequent depression and loneliness, her home had provided a stable presence, a safe refuge, and a warm embrace. She had spent more time and energy gardening, both as a way to heal and as a way to add beauty to her loving home.

As she thought about the article, it made sense to her that gardens could be powerful. She had an added motivation in that she cared about her city. It had provided her with schools for her children, police and fire protection, wonderful recreation areas, Como Park and Zoo, and a beautiful community center with a swimming pool. She wanted to give her city something beautiful.

Joan pulled all these thoughts into a plan. She would make her front garden a peace garden. She developed an idea to install a peace pole and surround it with stones decorated by the neighborhood children. A nearby nursery agreed to donate the stones, and the kids painted them with their names and flowers. Then one inspiring spring morning, they processed with the peace pole into the garden, while friends sang.

Many people walk by going to the bus stop and hundreds drive by every day. Many appreciate the garden. Joan says it is not uncommon for someone to stop to tell her how much he or she appreciates this space. Some say it brightens their day. One woman says a prayer each day she walks by. Last fall a man gave Joan a poem he'd written as he reflected on her garden. One son recently said that she has given a soul to this piece of the earth. In return, Joan is grateful that this city and home have given her a sense of place.

Why would this connectivity be so? The Native American culture has this understanding deeply embedded in its culture and could model this to our country. This is simply and beautifully summed up in the book, *The Sacred Tree,* "All things are interrelated. Everything in the universe is a part of a single whole. Everything is connected to everything else. It is, therefore, possible to understand something only if we can understand how it is connected to everything else." Gardens and nature help us learn these lessons.

We could give "yard" richer and more beautiful meanings. Our yards are our closest connection with nature. You may love going to a city, state or national park or to lakes, oceans, or mountains. We often think of that as nature. Our front and backyard nature is every bit as important, perhaps more so. You can't go to the other places every single day of your life; you can go in your yard, though. If you live in an apartment, you might have a few plants on your balcony or inside. You have limited influence on the public spaces, but you can steward your private space.

Another meaning we can give to our yards is to see them as our connective tissue or gateways to our neighbors and beyond them to the city. I remember the astronauts talking about how as they moved further and further out into space, they came to see that the boundaries that we think separate nations are really imaginary lines. In the big picture, the Earth was one organism.

Our concept of property is somewhat similar to the idea of national boundaries. It can be a useful distinction for some purposes, but for others it is meaningless. Our home is really part of a larger organism when we see that property lines are imaginary relative to various aspects of home. When it comes to creating simple beauty and a meaningful home, our neighborhood matters. A lovely home amidst disrepair of a whole block will have an effect. We can steward the earth right at home.

A sterile unfriendly neighborhood calls for meaningful

connections in a country where too many people are
"Bowling Alone" according to Robert Putman. We
can influence our neighbors and those visitors passing
through. After conducting 500,000 interviews, Putman
argues that we spend less time with family, friends, neighbors, and participating in civic organizations than we did
twenty-five years ago. The result is more impoverished
lives and less sense of community.

At one time in history, not that long ago, it was likely
that multiple generations lived together, and extended
family stayed within miles of where they were born.
Home was a powerful idea and a strong magnet. Today,
only about 37–50% of Americans live within fifty miles
of where they were born.

The trend to move away seems to be slowing, but that
still leaves many people who do not have family nearby.
Combined with the changing demographics of the aging
baby boomers and the need for new social networks is
clear. One place to find meaningful relationships and a
sense of community is in our neighborhoods.

When we first moved into our neighborhood, I knew
its political leanings, that it was safe, close to the lake
and creek, and a convenient location. We really hadn't
thought much more about the neighborhood beyond that.
If we had had children, I'm sure we would have been
more aware of other issues. Children can help bind neighbors together.

We were busy with work, friends, and extended family.
For a while we were focused on the inside of the house.
As we began to have the time to pay more attention to

the exterior, I realized that just as our house and yard needed some attention, so too, did the neighborhood.

Some homes were just fine. Others were beginning to show wear and tear. Some neighbors had been there long enough to have raised children and have see them leave. Perhaps they no longer noticed the fading colors and broken screens. Other neighbors were elderly. We wondered if they couldn't keep up their homes the way they once had.

We realized how few neighbors we had met, so we started taking walks after work or on weekends hoping to catch a glimpse and start a conversation. We did meet a few and did brief introductions, but it didn't seem as though there was much to say. At least we could put a face and name with a house.

It was only as we started doing more things in the yard, that we really started to meet people. Neighbors, as well as strangers, stopped and complimented the yard or asked about a flower or shrub. Or, we would trade pet stories as our dogs romped around the yard. Before I knew it, we were sharing and problem solving. They'd tell me where they lived and asked questions or told me their stories. Yards, gardens, pets, children, and human needs become the bonds to creating a community.

Bonding Elements

Our first real friend in the neighborhood was Grace, an elderly woman who lived across the alley from us. We "adopted" each other. I would visit and compliment her pet hobby—garage sale finds—whether they interested me or not. They pleased her, and that was what mattered.

She was widowed, did not have children, and was in her late seventies. She welcomed the company.

Bob handled the snow on her corner lot, in addition to our corner lot. She rewarded him with her seven layer salads and brownies. I climbed on her roof and cleaned out the gutters of pine needles. I was thanked with glasses of lemonade and more brownies. We did other yard work or some touch up painting.

She would keep us company and tell us stories about the neighborhood. A typical example was the Saturday she came over to my yard and said, "Put that paint brush down and come here. I bet you don't know about that alley." We went out in the alley, crossed the street to the south of us, and walked part way down that alley. Then we turned around and had a long view of the two connected alleys.

"What do you see?" she asked.

"A long alley with a big dip in it." I replied.

"What does the dip look like? Use your imagination," she instructed.

I tried to cooperate, despite being distracted by my thoughts about my paintbrush drying out and the grocery shopping I wanted to do. Finally, I laughed and said, "It would have made a good sliding hill when I was a kid."

Grace laughed at that, but it wasn't the right answer. "You need to think bigger, imagine a big picture," she said as she now steered me back toward the street, then turned and motioned that I should climb up on my other neighbor's grassy bank. "Look at the yards and imagine some of the houses gone in the middle of the block."

These occasional exercises of hers usually turned up interesting little gems of history, so I had learned to play along. Finally I began to have an idea of what she wanted me to see. "Was there a pond here at one time?" I asked in shock.

"So I was told," she said. "It was before my time, but I'm sure it's true." We continued to look at the contours of the land imagining where the shore would have been. When Bob returned home, we replayed the scenario for him.

Years later when I had a house history done, I told the historian about this theory. Sure enough, he found a map at the historical society from the mid-1800s that showed a pond right where we had imagined it to be. Grace was as excited as we were. She had stories about our house, about the days of the trolley cars, and more.

It was during Christmas season of 1981 that we last had her over for dinner. It had been a hard winter, and she seemed to be slowing down. She brought me a woven basket. On the cover was a small pink angel. She said it had been hers ever since she was a little girl. She wanted me to have it. It had been aged with love. The angel's pink skirts were full but faded, as was the face, and the wings were slightly tarnished with age. It was beautiful and touching. Along with it was a very meaningful note.

Grace died a few weeks into January during a bitterly cold storm with thigh-high snow. Her lights didn't come on when it got dark, and she didn't answer when I called. I decided I'd better go over. By the time I was bundled up and halfway across the alley, her porch light came on, and a man went in the house. An ambulance pulled up at the same time.

It was a friend's nephew. Grace and her friend checked in with each other every day. When the friend couldn't get through to Grace, she had called her nephew. We found Grace on the floor in the kitchen. She had died of a heart attack several hours earlier, and hit her head in the fall. The paramedics said she probably had died instantly.

I went home with a heavy heart and tears streaming down. Most of my grandparents died before I was born. I barely remember the surviving grandmother who died shortly after my mother. Bob had not had grandparents around either. Grace had been like a grandmother to us. Our relationship was simple, beautiful, and harmonious. We wish she had lived long enough for our daughter, Laura, to know her.

Building Community

One weekend I was in the yard and a senior citizen from down the block complimented me, "Glad you are taking those shrubs out. They have looked half dead for years." A couple weeks later, she stopped by one day when I was watering my new plants. "A funny thing happened when I got home from commenting on your shrubs. I realized mine looked kind of the same. Any ideas for something I can plant that won't cost too much? I haven't gardened much these past years."

Our yard was sufficient when we moved into the house. It had grass (and its share of weeds). The evergreen bushes were still functional. The bushes in the backyard were gorgeous in autumn. Between my job, working on the interior of the house, family and friends, we didn't have much time or money to put into the yard. We had some ideas about what we wanted and took small, incremental steps each year toward that vision. All the pieces would accumulate into something beautiful and harmonious.

Beauty in a yard can spread and create relationships with strangers. Another senior citizen had the honor of having lived on our block longest. She had been born in her house and inherited it when her parents died. She told me, "You always seem to be doing something. What's nice is that the somethings are little things that others can do, not big costly additions. The fresh paint or new flowers just make me smile and want to do something myself."

More years passed as my yard transformation continued. The number of women who stopped to talk increased as I worked in the yard and began to look more and more pregnant. We had a new topic to discuss. When Laura was born, and we took her outside, more attention came our way. One night a senior couple, Gwen and Don, stop by to see her. Gwen was a retired nurse and was delighted to take a crying baby in her lap and give her a soothing massage.

The following spring Laura was growing as well as my flowers. I began to receive occasional comments from neighbors telling me that we had started a rejuvenation of the neighborhood; our seven-year effort was bearing fruit. Deb, another newer homeowner at the other end of the block, was receiving similar feedback. The neighborhood seemed to be asking for a "remodel," both in physical appearance and in becoming a more welcoming place. That was going to take time and many small steps. Deb and I thought we would start small.

National Night Out was coming up in August. We organized the block to participate. Many people were grateful when we approached them with the petition to close off the street and have a potluck dinner. That went over pretty well. Turnout was good and food bountiful.

The next summer, Deb landscaped her backyard, so we arranged a Saturday morning tour of her yard, sweet rolls, and a plant swap. One summer evening, I served ice cream sundaes in our backyard as neighbors appreciated my garden's progress.

By the time Laura was in grade school, many of these had become annual events. She helped arrange for a Christmas food shelf collection at our house and played Christmas carols on the piano. She added the option of a donation to the humane society for those who forgot food. Pleasant relationships developed over the years at the same time that more yards and homes seemed to have beauty works in progress. Laura also became the go-to-person when people went on vacation and needed flowers watered or cats fed.

When Laura was about eleven years old, she developed an interest in photography. She wanted to have a big project, so we developed an idea of a block booklet with one page per house. She took a photo of each house and developed a few questions that went under the pictures. In addition to name, address, and phone, she asked about children, careers, interests, and how long the owners had lived there. Then, she went door-to-door until everyone on the block had completed the form. She created a simple house design on green paper for the cover.

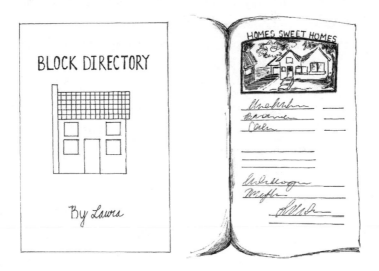

At the next block party each household received a copy in return for a contribution toward the photo and copying costs. To her delight, everyone raved about the booklet. Last year, about fifteen years since she made these, a new neighbor told me that she loved inheriting the booklet from the seller, even though it was getting out of date. Laura was touched that her project had been meaningful to others. She is now a homeowner and a block leader.

Our latest effort in simple beauty and meaningful connections has been a swing. We've had a bench swing on our back deck for a long time, but two years ago, we added one to the front yard. It sits in a small garden area off to the left of the front door. It's a woodland green color sitting amidst red mulch and flowers. Better yet, it is made of recycled milk bottles.

We wanted to use it as a way to send a message that said, "Feel free to stop by and say 'hello.'" Gardens and seating that are visible, rather than behind fences, offer an invitation, as well as providing a common reference point for starting a conversation.

Challenging Neighbors

All neighbors are not like Grace or Deb. Sometimes that connection is great and sometimes not. I've had both. Arguments can occur over property lines, parties, children, or pets. Sometimes our neighbors have grown up in different "soil" than we have, and there is a fundamental disconnect between appropriate behavior and flawed behavior.

When Athena died, we eventually got another dog for Laura and as a companion for Tasha. The new pup was a beautiful white American Eskimo. We named her "Amanda" since we seemed to have a pattern of names that ended with an "A." Her nickname quickly became Mandy.

It was one of "those" mornings. I had work that was due for a client the next day, and my daughter's part-time nanny was ill. I helped Laura start an activity, turned on the dishwasher, and headed to my office. Mandy frolicked by my side. About fifteen minutes later I remembered that I needed to take something out of the freezer for dinner.

Returning to the kitchen, I discover the dishwasher had overflowed. The floor looked like a small swimming pool. For the next while, I was busy calling for a service repairperson, drying up water, and trying to keep Mandy out of the water. I was frustrated, but Mandy was having a ball. I had to put her in the sink and rinse all the detergent of her legs. Laura thought it was quite funny. I was fortunate that Becky, a neighbor who now owned Grace's house, called to ask Laura along to the park with her two children.

When the repairperson rang the doorbell, the dogs started barking. Tasha responded to my command of "Quiet," but Mandy wasn't trained yet. I put her outside on her leash to be out of the way for a few minutes. I made it to the front door, let the repairman in, walked back to the kitchen, and was, at most, two minutes into the discussion when Tasha started growling. I ignored it until Mandy's bark suddenly turned into a horrible squeal of pain.

I raced out to find a stranger in our backyard with his hands around Mandy's neck. I took the steps in a leap and pulled her from the man's arms. We started yelling at each other as Mandy whimpered in my arms. She seemed all right, but scared. Just then, Becky and the kids came home to get some toys. Seeing the situation, Becky made a beeline for the house with the kids as I handed Mandy to her.

The stranger was shouting that I frequently leave my barking dogs outside all day. I was shouting that I do no such thing, and that he'd better get off my property and stay off. After a few more choice words on both sides, the man left, slamming my gate behind him. I was shaken; I walked back into the kitchen, slumping into a chair trying to figure out what had just happened. The repairman at least added a little comic relief. He had heard everything. He said, "I can't believe that guy. I was about to come out, but you had the situation so well in hand that I figured I'd just be in the way."

After checking on Mandy, Laura, and the neighbors, I called Bob, our attorney, and the police for some advice. Given that I didn't even know who this man was and hadn't had the presence of mind to watch which way he went, there didn't seem much to do.

Shortly after dinner, Becky called. She had been telling another neighbor what had happened. That neighbor had heard of a similar incident on her block. It turned out that the stranger was new to the neighborhood and she knew where he lived. Suddenly, my wonderful safe home and neighborhood seemed violated.

That lit a fire. Bob wanted to march over to the guy's house. That didn't sound good to me, so I reminded him about the advice from our attorney and the police. Instead I went straight to the computer and composed a strong threatening letter based on that advice. It castigated his reprehensible behavior and promised the wrath of the law if he ever stepped on our property again.

My memory is vivid of what happened next. I was standing in the dining room reading the letter to Bob for his input. After I finished, Bob was adding a couple points. Laura piped up, "Mommy, next time I see him, I'm going to tell him to leave Mandy alone and kick him," she said vehemently.

Bob and I looked at each other in shock. We were so engrossed in our fear and anger that we were not noticing what messages we were sending to our child. A whole new perspective entered the picture. This was not the behavior or values that we held dear and would want to teach her. What a wake up call that was.

We tore up the letter and tossed it, making sure Laura was once again watching and involved as we went down a new path. The next draft was firm but conciliatory. We acknowledged that barking dogs could be annoying. I explained that I worked out of the house and we had a part-time nanny. It was not our dogs that were barking all day. We asking that he call, or come over and talk, if he was annoyed with a barking dog. Then he could find out if it really was our dogs (among the ten on the block) that were the problem.

As I sat in my office rereading the letter, I thought about how much difference one's neighbors make to your sense of home. We lived in a pleasant, safe neighborhood. This incident made me think again about all those who live with much more violence at their doorstep than we had. I thought about all the children in the world who live in fear every day. At the end, I added an additional thought to the letter. It read, "I don't think we can ever have world peace if neighbors can't get along." I read it to Bob, with Laura in hearing range.

I delivered the letter through his mail slot. A few days later, after no response, I managed to get a little more information about him. He was single, worked at night, and went to school on the side. Evidently, he tried to sleep during odd times so barking dogs really annoyed him.

I kept an eye out for him wanting to get a response to the letter. One day he was cutting his grass. After that, he started planting a few flowers. This seemed like a different person. Trusting my instincts, I decided it was time to try talking. I explained a few things to Laura first and then took her by the hand as we walked to his house.

He did not look up, although, I was sure he saw us coming. "I'm your neighbor that left you a letter recently. Did you get it?" I asked. He continued to work pretending he hadn't heard me. When we didn't move, he finally looked up and said, "I thought of bringing cookies, but you probably would have thought that I had poisoned them." That broke the ice. I laughed a little and said, "Yes, I might have. Are you willing to do what I asked in the letter?"

"Sure. No problem," he replied. There was a long pause. "I never got a letter like that in my life, I showed it to my mom and my sister and some friends. They never saw anything like it either," he continued. He wrinkled his face quizzically and said, "Are you from that hippie generation? I mean, like, world peace? Nobody talks that way in real life. At least I didn't think so until now."

I laughed. "I guess we are from that generation, and we do try to remember to be that way." We left on that note. As we went home, I asked Laura how she felt now. She said, "I still don't like him, but I won't kick him." For myself, I had the strangest feeling that we had made a tiny movement forward in creating world peace. We never became friends, but we were at peace.

Others had some trouble with him, but we didn't. Eventually, he moved.

The incident had left an emotional scar on Mandy. Despite training, patience, and a dog expert, she became very territorial and aggressive. After some close calls, we had to have her put down. The hardest lesson was letting go and forgiving. We believe our thoughts, feelings, and intentions are cast out into the world, and have an effect on people and things around us. That helped.

When Disaster Hits

Having good relations with neighbors may become critical. Some day you may need each other for something larger than what one home can do. Aristotle said, "The city . . . is a partnership for living well." Perhaps we all need a reminder about that. Too often we leave it up to some level of government to make the environment a good one.

Disasters make the invisible connection we feel for each other become visible. As we try to rebuild, we are reminded of how many decisions and how much effort goes into making a home. The unusual combination of free assistance, diverse talents, but common vision and goals, leads to effective, productive, and loving accomplishments that no one could do alone. Nature provides examples of this. Milton Olson takes lessons from geese. He says, "Geese fly in formation with a common direction and a sense of community. This formation adds 71% greater flying range than if a bird flew alone." Our friends learned this from experience.

It was a Saturday evening, August 8. John and Lynne sat down with TV trays to eat dinner in the family room and watch a show on public television. Ella, their eight-year-old black lab, was on her bed nearby. They were aware that there had been a tornado watch in effect, but the weather outside their windows didn't seem to be changing.

Out of nowhere, they heard a tremendous roar, as if a train was bearing down on the house, and the patio doors started shaking unlike anything that had ever happened before. One of them called, "Get to the basement." They only made it about ten feet. They ended up on the floor but don't remember how they got there. John was on top of Lynne, trying to protect her. The trays and food were flying. Insulation was everywhere. John remembers a suction sound as the tornado passed.

It was over in seconds. They were all right. Then Lynne panicked. "Where is Ella?" They called her name and then saw her frozen to her bed. She responded to their calls and then stuck to them like glue for the next three months. When they stood up, they realized a big cross beam from the family room ceiling had come down and was lying parallel to them. Thank God, it had not landed on them.

There were holes in the ceilings filled with huge branches. There were so many trees down in their suburban backyard that they could not get out the back door. As they went out the front door, neighbors rushed to check on them.

The police and fire department came rapidly. They sent

the police to check on a missing elderly neighbor. Ella moved with John and Lynne like a shadow. They were in shock but grateful that they were safe. Everything seemed surreal. The sky was a strange inky color.

It was bizarre how the tornado had touched down so significantly and rapidly in one small area and then vanished. "It is one thing to know that can happen and another to experience it," they said. Other houses had to have roofs replaced due to wind damage, but no one else had trees actually on their homes. Some nearby homes were untouched. John and Lynne's home and property had taken a significant portion of the tornado hit.

Lynne called their two adult children and the insurance company. The power was out in the whole neighborhood. It was getting dark, so there wasn't too much anyone could do that night. John stayed in the house, but Ella and Lynne went to a neighbor's. Neither John nor Lynne slept much that night.

By Sunday morning, they realized people would ask to help, and they would have to say, "Yes." All that independence and "I'll do it myself" attitude goes away when something this big happens. They had had a heavily wooded lot in the back and on the sides of the house. One very large oak with a diameter of approximately three feet had come down on part of the back of the house. Two other large trees and some branches joined it. The entire back of the house had to be rebuilt. That included the family room, kitchen, dining room, living room, and the deck.

Later they said, "We knew we would have help, but

we have been touched at the generosity of family, friends, and total strangers. Now when we hear about someone else's disaster, we have a new desire to reach out and help. We also have learned more about how to do that."

They were amazed at the people who came to help, especially strangers. People dropped off bags of ice and bottles of water. Further down the street a neighbor, who they didn't know well, set up a sailboat and loaded it up like a smorgasbord with food and drinks for everyone.

After the biggest tree was removed from the house, they begged the tree service to place tarps over the roof, since they were so vulnerable. Even though the service had other large jobs lined up, they spent at least two extra hours covering the roof. As they worked, people showed up with more and more tarps. Within forty-eight hours after the tornado touchdown, their son, daughter, and a dozen other people were working with chainsaws to make a dent in their fallen forest.

Many were friends of their daughter. She did a great job coordinating everyone. Some were good friends and neighbors, but others were only casual acquaintances. The 70-year-old mother of a neighbor even helped haul brush. The husband of John's secretary, a professional woodcutter, stopped by with his commercial saw and cut for many hours.

They were very grateful for all this help. They worried about the liability if someone got hurt. "But there was no stopping anyone. We think there is something about testosterone and chain saws," they said. All the helpers seemed to have fun doing the heavy work, and there was a real sense of community. They only quit cutting when every chain saw become too dull to cut.

The city, too, was very helpful. They said that they would haul away all the trees and brush at no charge if it was stacked on the street in front of the house by Tuesday at 2:00. Two trees were so big there was no way to get them to the street, but the city brought in equipment and hauled them away despite that.

By Monday, they had hired a contractor and been reassured that the house could be rebuilt, but they had to get out within forty-eight hours. This meant getting a mover quickly and renting storage. Other neighbors now focused inside the house. They emptied the freezer and stored the food. Six neighbors packed up Lynne's kitchen. Her china was boxed and taken to a neighbor's for safe-keeping. Others brought food or had John and Lynne over for dinner. Helping hands seemed to be everywhere.

In the meantime, they had to find a place to live. They were fortunate in that area as well. An acquaintance of John's had a condo that was a second home, and it was available. It was hard to think about what to pack and take with them for three months. Everything else would be in storage and inaccessible.

They also learned what is not helpful. There were gawkers who got in the way. One woman walked uninvited into their destroyed living room and started asking lots of questions while they were trying to talk to the contractors. She seemed oblivious to how intrusive she was being. Uninvited and sometimes very pushy contractors showed up as early as 6:00 AM trying to promote themselves. They did not take "No," well at all. They ignored signs stating that a contractor had already been hired.

Another problem was the news media. From Saturday night through Monday, they set up big floodlights and kept trying to interview anyone who would talk to them. John and Lynne had other priorities and weren't in the mood for interviews. They also didn't want their names and information in the news.

Once they were past that first flurry of things, Lynne said she had time to mourn. "I noticed how I missed simple things like my sewing room and sitting on the deck looking at the trees. I hadn't realized how much I took the trees for granted and what they added to our home.

"The backyard and forest were our special place. After twenty years of planting, we had just gotten it the way we wanted it this past year. Now it was such a mess; that was really hard. All those tender plants that I had raised were smashed. There were huge ruts everywhere. Much of our canopy and many of the smaller ornamental trees were gone. You can imagine how many stacks of wood we have from thirteen trees. And now, I will have to design a sun garden, rather than my shade garden."

After moving through the feeling of being overwhelmed, they began to focus on putting their home back together. That was exciting. When the trusses and roof were replaced and the walls went up, they could see the progress. It started to take shape and began to look more like their home. All of this took time. John needed to maintain his law practice, so he would typically work until 3:30 or 4:00 and then come to the house. Luckily, Lynne could be available, as she would just turn down the substitute nursing opportunities during this period. It was a full time job to manage everything.

Then, they hit a new wave of being overwhelmed. There were so many decisions to make on doors, windows, woodwork, wiring, paint, insulation, and the list went on. It was a chance, however, to upgrade some things in the house. The contractor recommended a wider baseboard, so they went to a millwork place where there were many choices on little samples. Lynne liked them all. By the time they were to select paint colors, Lynne was so tired of making decisions that she told them to keep whatever colors were already in the rooms.

Fortunately, they had chosen a great contracting team who were knowledgeable and saw opportunities to enhance the house in ways that John and Lynne couldn't see. With the wrong people, they could see how this would have been a horrible experience.

"Among the big lessons learned," they said, "is the reality of how many big things can happen to you and your home over which you have no control. We thought of our home as a safe haven and that safety had been breached, but it could have been so much worse. We were lucky. Our home could be restored.

"We were touched by all the help and kindness we received. Home is larger than your physical dwelling. It includes the whole neighborhood and beyond. We didn't feel as if we lost our home because it was there, just badly hurt. Even when we had to move out, one of us was back at the house every day. Neighbors and relationships still connected us to our feeling of home."

Lynne and John's story can remind us of just how

much goes into making a home. When we have the leisure to build that home over years and even decades, it's a very different experience. We talked about how much worse it must be for people who get hurt or when someone is killed. Do their families want to leave or stay in the house? We talked about those who lose everything, for example, in a fire, flood, mudslide, or other disasters.

I continued to think about the issue of those uncontrollable events that can surprise us. My list of what I had done was incomplete of preparations and forethought. I have copies of some critical information in our safety deposit box including a digital record of everything in the house and of special pictures I wouldn't want to lose. There are emergency signs on the house doors that say "A cat lives here, please rescue her." We have a good insurance policy.

We have arranged for our daughter to be on our safety deposit box, so that she can get access to it if necessary. When we travel out of the country, we also give her a bank check as a safety precaution. We do have wills and health directives. I've decided I will make a New Year's resolution to look into this issue. I want to do a better job of protecting my home and those things that matter. In the meantime, I've at least done a little research to identify possible resources that are listed below.

What happens when your safe haven is not able to protect you? That, too, circled back to Lynne's comments about home is more than your dwelling. It is the loved ones in our lives who cannot be replaced. Just as the house has an exterior and an interior, so do we. It is our interior intangible values and spiritual beliefs that are our more enduring home.

Emergency Preparation Resources at bookstores or online
- *When Disaster Strikes Home! 101 Ways to Protect Your Family From Unthinkable Emergencies*
- *Organize for Disaster: Prepare Your Family and Your Home for Any Natural or Unnatural Disaster*
- *The Complete Idiot's Guide to Disaster Preparedness*
- American Red Cross website—search under preparedness fast facts for PDF files for many kinds of preparedness from storms to fire prevention to pet safety

Tied to the World

Our homes are tied to the world in many ways, most of them unseen. Trees are important to a house and a home. They provide beauty, a place to rest, to play, temperature control, pleasing sounds, and much more. At a global scale, they are like the lungs for our home planet. Planting a tree or caring for the trees you already have is a meaningful contribution to the world. Since we can't keep planting trees in our yard, we find it satisfying to make contributions to American Forests to plant new trees around our country and world.

The *Talmud*, a collection of ancient rabbinic writings about Jewish law and tradition, suggests that to be successful in life one should plant a tree, write a book, or have a child. What do these three elements share? They make a lasting contribution after we are gone. The tree stands out to me as having the greatest assurance of contribution. Many books are written that do not make a positive and lasting contribution. We have hopes for our children, but no guarantees.

More and more of us have friends or colleagues all over the world with whom we are connected by email. This is another invisible way that what we do at home is tied to our country and world. A Chinese friend with dual citizenship recently emailed me. She grew up in China but also has lived in Minnesota for many years. She is currently in China due to her job. She commented on how much she misses the quiet of her Minnesota home, nature, the changing seasons, and clean air to breathe. She feels stressed all the time. She says that Shanghai is noisy all day and all night due to the amount of building that is occurring, and there is constant dust everywhere. Her infant daughter has had some health issues. I wondered if there was a relationship between all these things.

Our personal health also is tied to others. A home is where we establish patterns for healthy or unhealthy living. A significant part of national health care costs could be avoided, if we took individual responsibility for how we care for our bodies and souls. We learn and put into practice the most important things we can do for our physical and emotional health at home. That includes what we eat and drink, how we sleep, the degree of exercise we get, and how we live as spiritual beings. In addition, much of what is in our homes comes from all over the world.

In *The Blue Zones: Lessons for Living Longer From the People Who've Lived the Longest,* author Dan Buettner shares the results of his research in four different areas around the world whose people have the longest life spans. These people don't just live lives of 100 or more years but are vital and contributing members of society. He compiles a cross-cultural list of the nine best practices that matter in enhancing longevity. Interestingly, the vast majority of these practices are things we do or could learn to do in our homes. Having a sense of purpose and desire to contribute are among these important practices. His website—bluezones.com—has an informative self-assessment called the "Vitality Compass." It calculates life expectancy related to whether you engage in these healthy practices or not.

The decisions we make to do them or to not do them are often seen as personal choices; that is partially true. It is also true that when someone else develops an illness closely associated with an unhealthy life style, that person's decisions have costs associated with their treatment that then add to the cost of other peoples' health care coverage. So taking care of ourselves is also taking care of others. The conversations that could help our country become more united would include the need for individual freedom, coupled with responsibility for others, and compassion with accountability.

My experience many years ago as a high school social studies teacher informed me about our nation. I taught a government class called Rights and Responsibilities of Eighteen-Year-Olds. I noticed that my students were very interested in their rights and the rights of their friends, but they were not very interested in their responsibilities or in the rights of people who weren't their friends. I tried to help them see that you cannot have one without the other.

Many of the political conflicts we have today are between those who are rights focused and those who are responsibility focused. One version of rights focused wants government to stay small and contained, so they are free as individuals. Another version of rights focused are those who believe that almost everything is a right, and government needs to see to it that everyone has the same rights. Those who are responsibility focused want to bring accountability into the conversation. Right now, most of the arguments are positioned as either-or, right or wrong. I believe each group has a legitimate part of the truth.

The debate rages on big issues. At home, we consciously or unconsciously vote with our behaviors and daily decisions about how we eat, shop, exercise, contribute, spend our time, and how we sustain our community. I have learned to shop differently and bring my cloth bags. We belong to a community supported agricultural group from whom I receive all my organic summer vegetables. It is a non-profit rural community living and working with people with special needs, so my one act of membership supports multiple values and interests of mine. Your interaction with nature matters in your every day existence from food to gardens to your lawn.

Humans appreciate the greenery of grass and the cool tickle of it under our feet. Bare feet are a pleasure. I feel guilty, however, since grass requires care that is not environmentally sound. Fertilizers, weed killers, and the amount of water that it consumes are issues. Those chemicals find their way into rivers, creeks, lakes, and someone else's drinking water. Whatever happens in my yard, affects others. Many of us want to create a win-win for the earth and ourselves.

One step you can take is to expand your gardens or wooded areas reducing the grass space. The expansion of the gardens is especially beneficial to you if you are struggling to grow grass due to too much or too little sun or poor soil. My shade plants are thriving, don't require the same amount of water or fertilizer, no weed killers, and are much more interesting. This can be a long process of one area at a time year after year. If you have boulevards that roast under the intense summer sun, add a rain garden or more native plants at the ends of the boulevards or even the whole stretch. Along the way, you will benefit your body with the exercise.

An exhibit at the University of Minnesota Landscape Arboretum has inspired me regarding my next step. They were working with the theme of water. A large exhibit displayed new kinds of grasses that were emerging from their research. Signs explained the differences in water consumption, fertilization, number of mowings per season, and type of activity the grass could sustain. It allowed you to see and touch the grass while absorbing the information. I left convinced I could have less work, save money, and do the right thing. You can ask your local garden store for advice.

I was also reassured that I didn't need to start digging up portions of the lawn and start all over again with sod or seed. That thought could be discouraging. The process is much easier than you might have imagined. The recommendation is to make the transition over a three-year period. Put down new seed on top of your current lawn and cut back on watering and fertilizing. The new grass will replace the old relatively seamlessly. The rule of thumb is: change the habitat; change the plants. Sounds like a good prescription for human beings as well. If we want to change people, we could start with our human habitat.

Our yards also connect us to the larger world in another way. In a democracy, many use them as a place to voice their political opinions and try to influence others. At times, the yard signs we see are for candidates, but other times they are about issues. It might be a local school-funding topic, or it might be an expression supporting or contesting a potential war or supporting the troops. Regardless of your position, a good marketing person will tell you that if you want to influence anyone, stay respectful. Hopefully, the sign can express your deepest desire in a manner that is consistent with the rest of the life of the home.

After the 9/11 Attack on the World Trade Center, like most U.S. citizens, we were in shock. At first, our whole focus was on our country—our larger home in the world. It might have been one of the best uses of emails up to that point. Millions of messages sought or offered reassurances about the well-being of family and friends. Colleagues, customers, and suppliers around the world stopped business to inquire as well. The television in our homes showed people around the world lighting candles. We wanted to make a small statement in addition to sending donations. We finally decided to put our United States flag by the front door.

As we listened more closely over the coming days and watched as the world came together in grief, it became clear this was larger than Americans. The World Trade Center had been a place of global mingling, so those who died or were injured came from many lands. I began alternating my U.S. flag with my flag of the Earth in a small effort to say I care about all those affected.

Soon after, I found a note in my mailbox. It read, "Your Earth flag is so meaningful to me. I have felt alone. I, too, want to think about the whole world. You gave me hope. Could you call and tell me where to get a flag like yours?" Over the next few weeks, I had another person come to the door with the same question and a couple cars stopped when I was in the yard. It was a small thing, but it was meaningful to some of us.

When homes feel abundant in love and beauty, the home seems to want to share its abundance. A recent Parade Magazine survey revealed that Americans are increasingly interested in giving both time and money. About 94% believe it is important to support causes in our communities and 91% in the world at large. Almost half of those surveyed wanted to help strengthen their neighborhoods.

It doesn't matter what your financial resources are; it is the wealth of the spirit that is the deciding factor. Daniela and Alfonso are sister and brother. They have become U.S. citizens but have many family members still in Costa Rica. They are both in minimum wage jobs, but every paycheck has a portion that is sent home to help their families.

Since home is where we teach values, generosity is one value that is particularly easy to model. You could have a rule of thumb about allowances. Perhaps one-third is allotted each to spending, saving, and giving. Thanksgiving and other holidays are good times to involve children in donating and gift giving.

Traditionally, giving had been about time, talent, or money. Giving might be helping your own extended family, or your child's school, as well as donating to your church or other favorite organizations. Significant global events like the tsunami in Thailand or an earthquake also tend to open people's hearts and wallets. Or it may be a local event like the I-35W bridge collapse in Minneapolis. It is amazing the diversity of things one might want to support. Jolene has many interests and limited resources. She spends the better part of a weekend every year allocating her modest contributions among about forty organizations. She prefers to give a small amount to many organizations that represent her values.

Sponsoring organizations are getting more creative about offering us new ways to give. We can sit in our homes, peruse catalogs, and use the Internet to make personal choices. Heifer International's catalog allows you to buy animals for villages around the world and give it as a gift in someone else's name. If you want to give something to someone who really doesn't need anything, you can donate on your friend's behalf. I was pleased this Christmas, when my daughter gave me the gift of her donation of chicks to a Heifer sponsored village. I had modeled that to her for many years.

Kelsey is twenty-four and earns about $30,000 a year. She contributes to her church through an automatic payment plan. She also is exploring the new non-profit websites that she read about in an article called, "Three Charity Sites That Let Donors Call the Shots." Small donors have traditionally not had any control over how an organization spends the funds once the donation is made. These new organizations are changing that.

Kelsey likes the idea of choosing a specific use for her contribution, rather than only an organization. She also likes being able to track what happens after she has made her gift. She is exploring all three organizations mentioned in the article. GlobalGiving.org sponsors projects of many kinds around the world. Kiva.org allows donors to finance microloans to entrepreneurs in poor countries. DonorsChoose.org focuses on money and supplies for public school classrooms.

This past year Minnesota's non-profits and schools combined forces. They created a Give to the Max Day. In just one day, more than $14 million was raised for 3,434 Minnesota non-profits during the first event of this kind. There were matching funds for some contributions. More than 38,000 donors participated in the day of giving. When you know that you are combining forces with people all across your state, there is a different kind of excitement and sense of belonging. Friends and colleagues called, emailed, or texted each other asking if they had heard of this opportunity.

Carleen Rhodes, president and CEO of The Minnesota Community Foundation, The Saint Paul Foundation, and a sponsor of Give to the Max Day summed it up, "We are absolutely thrilled with the tremendous response Give to the Max Day received. We raised more than three times as much money for Minnesota non-profits than any other previous online community fundraising event in the United States. We look forward to continuing to help advance charitable giving in the Internet age through GiveMN."

Sometimes, resources aren't the issue. You have all the money you need, a huge home, or maybe two, with walk-in closets, and a three-car garage. You have money and room for forty pairs of shoes. Then the questions are different. Are you happy? Will more of anything make you happier? Do you want to use your resources to spread more happiness around to others?

Senior citizens have wisdom to share about happy and meaningful lives. Eric, a high-level executive, read some research about surveys of seniors who discussed the idea that no one on their deathbed said that they wished they had worked longer hours, made more money, or bought another house. He realized he had enough material well-being, but not enough human contact, nor enough satisfaction from being of service. He spread his financial wealth around already, but he wanted to do that with his time and skills as well.

One of his activities is tutoring math at a nearby community center. He ran into another retiree from his former business. She was also tutoring. Julie had worked on the factory line for years and had learned a lot of math when the company began doing more quality control. Now, they were both giving back in a similar way.

Fran has a disability. She says she decided to stop feeling

sorry for herself. So many people were helping her out that she felt like an invalid. She wanted to be able to give to someone else. Many types of volunteering were too demanding for her. One thing she could still do was drive within about a ten-mile radius of home. She decided to focus on her own neighbors. Now she drives people to doctor appointments or to do errands and feels useful.

Life at home seems more rewarding when this spirit is alive in them.

~

Reflections/Suggestions for Another Day:
• How does your home see property lines – as important or as imaginary lines?
• How have you affected your neighborhood or city?
• Have your neighbors done things that you appreciate?
• How do you feel about your neighbors? Are they part of home?
• What is the role of children in connecting a neighborhood?
• How is your neighborhood important to your child?
• What can you find out about the history of your area?
• What would happen to you if a tornado struck your home?
• How do you and your home connect to and contribute to the larger world?
• Have you considered what percent of your contribution you want to be personal? Local? National? Global?

Wrapped in Harmony

In *Home—A Short History of An Idea,* author Witold
Rybczynski describes the evolution of home and family
life, and how that parallels the development of the inner
life of human beings. Alluding to the fourteenth century,
he says, "Life was a public affair, and just as one did not
have a strongly developed self-consciousness, one did not
have a room of one's own." Rybczynski discusses how
privacy was unknown both in a physical sense and in an
interior conceptual sense in the person.

You might return to your tour of the 14th century
that we did in chapter one. Sleep and sexuality are two
aspects of life that would provide you with data about
privacy. You might be quite uncomfortable—physically
and emotionally. There weren't separate bedrooms,
just the one big hall. You might sleep in a chest or on
an upturned table. Real beds were very large—ten feet
square. Four couples could sleep next to each other.
Almost anyone slept anywhere. Children might be with
parents or strangers.

Three hundred years later, in the 17th century, you might be more comfortable as the march toward new concepts of home, family, and privacy were advancing across northern Europe. Valerie Suransky Polakow, in the *Erosion of Childhood*, identifies this as a watershed time for a new notion of childhood. The idea that childhood was a developmental stage that lasted beyond the age of seven was a whole new way of thinking. Until this idea emerged, children of all classes were pretty much considered adults at the age of seven and often sent off to work, apprenticeships, or in service to the church or military.

More intimate spaces were developing, separating public and private areas. Sleeping arrangements were changing. Several historians of home furnishings have discussed the idea that the awareness of a concern about the interior of the home—furnishings, privacy, and beauty—is much deeper than a material shift. In reality, it is an external manifestation of the development of the inner life of the person as an individual, as a couple, and as a family.

These developments were particularly strong in the Netherlands. Homes were smaller with fewer than six occupants. Work establishments were physically separate from the home. The Dutch had a level of prosperity that allowed this.

They also had a cultural value around independence that had significant ramifications. Having servants was looked down upon while self-employment was a virtue. Motherhood focused on raising one's own children rather than leaving it to servants, nurses, or governesses so a different kind of bond developed in the family. Most children lived at home until they were ready to marry and establish their own homes. This created a whole new relationship between parent and child.

Rybczynski sums it up eloquently. "'Home' brought together the meanings of home and of household, of dwelling and of refuge, of ownership and of affection. 'Home' meant the house, but also everything that was in it and around it as well as the people, and a sense of satisfaction and contentment that all these conveyed."

Desiring Unity

Human beings have an inherent spiritual need for unity. By 'spiritual' I do not mean religious. Religions are about dogma and practices of a group of people. Spirituality is an orientation towards life that recognizes a sacredness that may or may not be associated with God or a religion. There is a focus on the search for what has a depth of meaning aimed at the highest good and aligning oneself with that in daily living.

We want to fit, to belong, and to be united, especially in a meaningful cause. That cause could be significant or could be a winning team each of which will rouse our spirits in a different way. For those brief moments, we transcend ourselves and feel as if we are in it together. We also want this within our home and with anyone who enters it, as well as the neighbors who surround us.

When a home is wrapped in harmony, it doesn't mean the cessation of all conflict. We aren't built that way. Some days we just wake up ready to argue. Harmony means there is the desire to create and use known paths for re-establishing unity when conflict does arise. Your home provides many opportunities to practice this, so that when there is conflict about significant issues of relationships, kids, parents, or careers, you will have a foundation for resolution.

There are many books about communication and conflict resolution. One of the best is, *Nonviolent Communication: A Language of Life,* by Marshall Rosenberg. My desire in this book is to look at the dynamics of home that help create unity and harmony.

Each major element of creating a home can help restore its integrity when it gets out of balance. A home that is conceived in love will have shared values that are at its center. A home that is nurtured by beauty will provide a calming influence and help elevate the conversation. If you have used your creativity to enhance your home, you can bring that same capacity to the disagreement. When stories surround you, that shared history is a resource for understanding what is going on. If you have had your values tested and stayed in your integrity, you have lessons to draw upon. Which of these will help you depends on your situation.

There is more to the story of my desire to move to a new house and Bob's refusal to consider that. The debate lasted a couple of years, so over that time I had tried a variety of approaches that didn't work. I also began to learn how my home nurtures conversations. This is increasingly important given the rise in divorce rates and the 30% increase over the last decade in the number of family households with multigenerational living.

I tried the thinking-out-loud approach. That was a disaster. I tried the factual, logical approach, documented costs, and a history of our house investments. That led to a debate over some of the facts. Neither of us gained any ground. Next came the "Let's just look around." He had no interest. At times I was reasonable, sweet, engaging. Other times I was objective and logical, and then there were days when I was demanding and angry. Often these conversations occurred at random moments.

One Saturday I was sitting at the dining room table feeling stuck. Why couldn't I get through to him? We loved one another, so it shouldn't be so hard to communicate. A bouquet of flowers from Bob adorned the table. My home sneaked up on me and offered help. A memory flashed back. We were sitting at this same table. I didn't remember what we were discussing, but he said with frustration, "Just give me something to read so I can think."

It was like a light bulb going on for me. Bob processes data better when it is written rather than verbal. It removes the verbal overload and the emotional element. Neither mode is better; we just are different. This is true for many couples. Since the memory was so helpful, I let other stories come to mind about how we had reached agreement on other things. I was searching for the patterns of how we created harmony.

I wrote him a letter with my long list of logical reasons combined with my passion. That would allow him time to digest what I had to say. I also changed the request. Instead of asking him to move, I asked him to agree to consider a few houses. Then I would feel that he had been fair. I noticed that we had not discussed what values should help us through this conflict. I also realized he needed time to think, so it would be wiser to agree on a specific time to talk.

That was a turning point in our conflict. He read what I had to say and had time to think about it. He responded to my call for fairness, which was important to him. Setting a specific time to talk also took away any feeling of being ambushed or caught off guard. He said that if I could find houses that I really was excited about, in a given price range, then he thought it was fair that he be willing to look at them. My persistence was a tangible sign to him of how much this mattered to me.

As you know from my earlier story, we did not move. I couldn't find a home we liked better. Due to this change in how we communicated, however, I never felt as if I had lost the conflict. In fact, we both had won. Bob had known, in his own way, that this home had all we needed. We started a different conversation. Could we agree to invest in not only maintenance but also in making our functional home more beautiful? That would meet my real need, as opposed to, my perceived need. Bob was whole-heartedly in support of that. We were in harmony once more.

Things just seemed to fall into place after that in wonderful ways. The experience reminded me of a favorite quote from Anne Morrow Lindbergh in *Gift from the Sea,* "I want to 'live in grace' as much of the time as possible . . . I believe most people are aware of various periods in their lives when they seem to be 'in grace' and other periods when they feel 'out of grace' even though they may use different words to describe these states. In the first happy condition, one seems to carry all one's task before one lightly; as if borne along on a great tide; and in the opposite state one can hardly tie a shoestring."

In hindsight, my home was inspiring me through this process. The appeal to the value of fairness was critical. It is one of the core values of our home. Sitting in the beauty of my dining room looking at the flowers reminded me of the stories infused in our life together which gave me insight about how to communicate. The years of creative endeavors served me well in realizing I should ask for something that was a smaller and an easier step to take.

The next time you have a conflict you may want to enlist the aid of your home. Every situation is different and the specific solutions will vary, but the elements of home can be drawn upon in all cases. Even the furniture and arrangement of your home can contribute to reducing conflict and increasing harmony.

Sometime after Laura was married, she and Joe bought a house. Rather than have them incur more expenses, we decided to give them most of our living room furniture and a few other things. Then we would buy new things for ourselves. We were ready for a change. They took Laura's piano, our sofa, three living room chairs, a coffee table, two floor lamps, and a bookcase.

The question was not only what furniture to get, but now we also had new questions. We have a long living room that is divided by natural "pathways." Did we want to keep those and, if so, deal with them any differently?

With the piano gone that opened up new opportunities for the space by the fireplace. What did we to do with that? What did we want to stay the same? With just the two of us home, how would life change? What lighting would create more warmth? Homes need intimate spaces as well as entertaining spaces for larger gatherings. We could enhance those spaces with our new decisions, if we were thoughtful about harmony.

For me, the prime purpose of furniture is to provide inviting places for conversations. That means the arrangement of the furniture varies for small and large groups. Other times it means to reduce the quantity or rearrange the furniture to enhance standing space or movement space as people drift from one conversation to another. All these questions became part of our thought process as we shopped.

We have a Vermont Casting insert fireplace that we purchased about ten years ago. It is an efficient carefully engineered unit that doesn't waste heat like a traditional fireplace and is more environmentally sound. Before, there was one chair and the piano by the fireplace. Now that it sat empty, it seemed like a good spot for a new focus.

The purchase of two matching chairs for this area was pleasing. They rock, recline, swivel, and sit still. We have them placed facing the fireplace creating a new intimate spot for two. Once we are home and dinner is in the oven, we recline there and discuss our day. I also like to read or journal in this cozy spot. Depending on the weather, there is a real fire going or one in our imagination. There is something about fire as one of the basic

elements that touches our inner being. When we are
having a large gathering, we can easily swivel the chairs,
so they become part of a large group conversation area
facing the other direction.

Sounds of Home

All sounds can enhance or destroy harmony. The most
important sounds in a home are the voices that ring
through the environment. How do the voices in your
home sound to your ears? How would they sound to a
stranger? Are the voices that you hear, the voices of those
who live there, or the digitized voices of someone you
don't know? Think about which sounds are heard most
frequently—laughter, conversation, bantering, or shouting, swearing, or criticism.

The second most important sound is the balance
between activity noise and the sounds of silence.

Without the balance of quiet interspersed throughout the day, not just when everyone is sleeping, our systems go into overload and meaningful thoughts and actions slip away. The need for privacy, which as we saw earlier is in direct correlation to developing our inner world, is often related to sound.

In *The Geography of Home,* culture writer Akiko Busch observes, "Often, it seems, privacy is defined not by space, but by a specific activity such as reading, gardening, or taking a walk . . . it is often negotiated by controlling sound. Music, for example, may be the means to find peace." Music is important, especially the music our children and teenagers absorb because it affects their moods and values. Music does speak to our hearts and souls, as well as, our minds. What message is your home giving?

Television, computer games, and all other noisemakers have their place and function. What role are they playing in your home? Do they add to beauty and harmony and contribute to a better family and home, or do they detract, or are they neutral? How much of your life is being given to them? If you didn't have them, what would you be doing instead? What is your happy medium?

My favorite sounds? Quiet conversations, the trickle of water over the small stone pebbles in my water fountain, and my 1960s and 1970s music when I exercise. I am usually reading a book (and I do like the sound of turning pages) while others are watching TV. Wherever I am, though, I pause to smile when I hear Laura, Joe, and Bob's laughter when they watch a funny show.

The purring of a kitten and happy welcome of a dog please me. I like Christmas carols or Handel's *Messiah* playing when we decorate the tree. When I work, a CD called *Brainwave Symphony* heightens my concentration and creativity.

The sound of languages in a home is important as well. Rumi says, "All language is a longing for home." My father spoke Croatian and English, but I was to only learn English. I regret that. I think he had experienced so much discrimination in hiring, in being cheated when he would try to buy a car, or just cruel words thrown his direction for no reason at all, that he thought he was protecting me. Languages allow us to experience the world in different ways. They also are great brain developers. Given our global society, those who can speak different languages have an advantage.

Edie feels truly at home when she hears her native German spoken. She says that languages trigger emotions and deep childhood memories. She looks forward to every trip to Germany. What surprised her was to discover that the area of Mexico where she spends her winters has a German community, so she speaks as much German in Mexico a she does Spanish. Our friend, Victor, explains that while he can translate a story from Spanish to English or vice versa, it is never quite the same story because the languages contain different cultures.

There are many kinds of languages even within English. There are British, American, Canadian, and Australian English. There are also the languages of science, medicine, and poetry. Mathematics is universal. Then there are all the 7000 plus world languages. No one really knows how many there are because we keep finding more. Many are in danger of extinction.

Should that happen, we would have lost something because every language has its own wisdom. There are clashes going on around the world over the issues of language. A family needs to have things in common that bind them, and they need to respect the diversity of each member of the family. So too, in a nation and a world. Perhaps the family points a path toward both diversity and unity. Perhaps we need a common language and second languages to be the norm.

Dorwatha came from an Army family that moved every eighteen months. She is black but has white great-grandparents on both sides of her family and a prominent Cherokee Indian in her family tree. She also lived in the South and with Southern parents, so that shaped who she is. When she describes her home, though, it is often about the things that were the constants in her life. One example was, "a place where love was music."

Her mom did not work outside the home, so the house was her domain. She sang all the time as she worked. She'd sing black spirituals in a loud voice, and when the work got especially taxing, she prayed aloud as well "Lord have mercy!" "Oh Lord . . .Precious Jesus! Take me by the hand Lord!" and then she'd break into a song: "Precious Lord. Take my hand. Lead me on. Let me stand. I am weak. I am tired. I am worn . . ."

Daily her father would come home and put music on his reel-to-reel tape player. They would move through the world of jazz with Count Basie and Dizzy Gillespie. They'd hear Ray Charles and the Supremes, The Jackson Five, Rogers and Hammerstein, and so much more. Dorwatha looked forward to her father's arrival because the tunes would roll around the house and uplift everyone. No one ever had a problem as his music played. It was smiles, relaxation, and sharing about the day's activities.

They watched all of the Rogers and Hammerstein musicals and learned how to dance along with them and sing every word. Her oldest sister taught the youngest two of the six sisters how to hula. They would go to the living room and put on grass skirts, listen to a record, and swaying they would go. Sometimes all six would line up and sing songs, and their grandmother would dream that they had made it big in the music industry like the Lennon Sisters. She encouraged their singing.

Sometimes everyone came to the living room just to dance—soul dance. Shake their bodies to the syncopated beats of soul brothers and soul sisters crooning out tunes on the record player—Aretha Franklin, Isaac Hayes, James Brown, Dionne Warwick, and The Commodores. Her aunt would walk in the door and dance step to the beat into the room where the girls were shimmering and laughing. They would just laugh and dance totally outrageously until they were worn out. They all took piano and dance lessons, usually tap and ballet. The sounds of music and dance filled the air.

A researcher in Japan is interested in sounds, harmony, and human happiness. His name is Masaru Emoto, and he is the author of *The Messages of Water*.

In an effort to understand what was common to all human beings, he realized that it was water. Our bodies are mainly water. When we are born we are 90% water, and by the time we die we might be 50% water. He realized that the quality of that water in our inner landscape must have an impact on our health and well-being.

He and his assistants conducted many experiments exploring the influence of sound, written words, and prayer on the water. The vibration of music was the first experiment. Photography of ice crystallization patterns emerged after the water was exposed to music and then put through a freezing process. This gave him the visual information for which he was searching. He reports that, "Beethoven's *Pastoral Symphony,* with its bright and clear notes, resulted in beautiful and well-formed crystals. Mozart's *40th Symphony,* a graceful prayer to beauty, created crystals that were delicate and elegant. . . . In contrast, the water exposed to violent heavy metal music resulted in fragmented and malformed crystals at best."

His research continued as he tried a specific technique for freezing the bottles of water with words written on them. Words like *love, goodness,* and *thank you* created beautiful diverse patterns. Words like *hate, ugly,* and *fool* resulted in ugly deformed crystals. Love and gratitude were the two most powerful words in his study. There is much more to his research than can be reported here, but the message is that the sounds and words in our homes matter a great deal to what happens inside of us. Of course, we knew that, but this is an amazing confirmation.

What This Garden Will Grow

Have you ever had a dream or picture in your mind of how you wanted something to look? It might have been a room, a house, a garden, or then again it might be how you want to look, or how you want someone else to look. Maybe you wanted something to behave a certain way—some difficult shrub, your career, child, spouse, or neighbor. When you didn't get your way, you probably were feeling anything but harmonious.

Gardens are wonderful teachers about harmony. A big lesson is to pay more attention to what your soil will grow, and a bigger lesson yet is to accept what it will not grow. Then apply that lesson to everything and everyone else related to your home and work.

Once I was ready to start investing time in my yard, I began by replacing some woody evergreens in the front yard. I did not have much experience with gardening, so I sought the help of the experts at the local garden stores. I even took pictures to them of the areas in question and measured the amount of sunlight. I wanted to do everything right.

I was particularly interested in bushes that were supposed to be hard to kill. Despite my best efforts, many of them died within a few years. If something lived, it often was lackluster. I'd try again. For a little while things would look better but then die back.

I tried other corners of the yard with about the same results. Not even grass would grow in one part of the backyard. Eventually, we covered it with a deck for the turtle sandbox and plastic fort. It also made a great stage for the kids' plays for a while. This went on for 10 or 15 years.

The mother of one of Laura's friend's was a Master Gardener. It was time to hire a pro to actually come in the yard and help me. Kim walked around the yard and listened to my tale of woe. She talked a lot about the soil and took samples to send to the University of Minnesota Extension Service.

Then she walked around the house looking *up*. That surprised me. She pointed out that my large overhangs were preventing the rain from getting to plants close to the house. Some of my problems could be moisture deficiency. Then she asked if I knew what my trees were. I did know. They were black walnuts. She informed me that my soil problems were probably due to the toxicity that these trees release into the soil. I already had a love hate relationship with those trees. This news did not help.

Black walnuts have a large and lovely crown, which provides nice shade, but they are messy. They drop fuzzy worm-like things in the spring that stain. In late summer and fall they drop millions of walnuts. (OK, maybe tens of thousands.) They stain badly and when broken open the shells can pierce bare feet. In heavy seasons, I rake the yard weekly to clean them up, and that is before the leaves and their long stems start to fall. If anyone tells you they are worth a great deal of money because walnut makes lovely furniture, do more research; there is more to the picture. We were not in harmony with our trees, and our trees were not in harmony with most of the things I wanted to plant.

Adding insult to injury, were the squirrels. They love walnuts. They are attracted to our yard from miles away. We have had the roof repaired six times because they gnawed their way in to create a storage area for the walnuts. We had the inner storage area of the attic screened in after they began gnawing their way into some of the clothing storage boxes and selecting fabric to line their nests. When we had the aluminum fascia removed three years ago, old shells thundered down almost knocking the roofer off his ladder. They filled three large garbage cans. In desperation, we had squirrels trapped and removed to distant lands.

Bob thought it was funny to let the dogs out to chase squirrels that were sitting on the deck eating away. The squirrels paid him back. Bob can testify that a cluster of walnuts dropped by an angry squirrel on the top of your head can drive a strong man almost to his knees.

I was told to use the walnuts for baking. A squirrel's bite can exceed 7000 psi (pounds per square inch). In comparison, a human's bite is around 150 psi. Thus, a squirrel's bite is about 50 times as strong as a human's. No wonder I needed a hammer and chisel to open the walnuts and gave up.

Once I had exhausted my complaints, Kim gave me a quick lesson about ecosystems and environments that was to have a much larger impact on me than she could have imagined. Plants adversely affected by being grown near black walnut trees exhibit symptoms such as yellowing, wilting, and eventual death. (That sounded very familiar to me.) The problem is a chemical called "juglone" which occurs naturally in all parts of the tree. Juglone has experimentally been shown to be a respiration inhibitor depriving sensitive plants of needed energy for metabolic activity. (Great, I have trees that suffocate plants in addition to driving me crazy.)

While many plants grow well in proximity to black walnut, there are many more whose growth is hindered. Kim suggested I use the Internet and do two things. One was to read about juglone and the other was to get a list of plants compatible with the trees. Other plants and trees have their own version of this, so read on for the more general lesson.

What I read reminded me of humans as well as plants. Both plants and animals compete to assure a place in nature. Competition, by definition, takes one of two forms—exploitation or interference. Plants will compete for sunlight, water, and nutrients and, like animals, for territory just as people do for attention, resources, and space. This influences the distribution and amount of organisms in an ecosystem. It is similar to how members of a household—plus their friends and things—carve up the space of the home. The interactions of ecosystems define an environment just as the interactions of the people and their stuff defines your home.

If size is a symbol of power, then my trees would definitely win and my plants lose. I went on to Kim's second assignment. She said to select plants I liked, and she would help me do a plan for the yard. I discovered that the ones that grew well were mainly shade plants with limited color and size. That was the opposite of what the image in my mind wanted.

I took a number of lessons away from this. They apply to my home life as well as my understanding of people at work, in politics, and life in general. One was how hard it was to let go of my preconceived idea of how things ought to be. My soil just could not grow some of the things that I wanted. Soil could also be a metaphor for our human soil—biological, intellectual, spiritual, and sociological. That was true as a parent, in my career, and in other relationships. Without changing the "soil" of people and organizations, we can't change the fruits they bear. I discovered new beauty that was much simpler to attain when I learned to let go.

The second lesson was to appreciate what I had, as well as, what I didn't have. Some examples were my discovery of Annabelle Hydrangeas, Bleeding Hearts, and Snakeroot. They love my soil. My cousin, Mike, loves Bleeding Hearts. He has friends who own a garden center. Mike helps them out on holiday weekends so has learned a lot about plants. He says he has never seen such big Bleeding Heart plants. He is amazed by how much longer mine stay green before turning yellow and dying back in late summer.

As a former teacher, and as a parent, I've seen how parents have both conscious and unconscious expectations of their children that cannot be met. The effort to grow their children into something incompatible with the child's true nature causes pain. Although they don't mean to do this and don't think of it this way, that is what is happening, and the children feel it. The soul (soil) of the child suffers by trying to produce a result (fruit) that it was not meant to bear. Focus on their gifts, not your desires.

I've done the same thing to myself in career goal setting and have now learned to see myself in new ways. I gave up one set of goals and realized that writing and coaching were a much better fit for the soil of who I am. Without that change, I would have forfeited writing a book like this and the immense joy of bearing this fruit. I've learned to coach other people through a similar discovery.

One of my favorite, successful, and recognized CEOs is Chuck Denny. He has been recognized for his leadership, insight, and efforts to turnaround his company, to bring executive compensation into a more ethical framework, assist many of the major institutions of Minnesota as well as the national Alzheimer's Association, and write an international code of ethics for business called the Caux Round Table Principles. Yet, even he described his own process this way:

"We're all conditioned by society to prefer certain paths and goals. We notice that success in this world is defined by following some career track, so that is where we want to go. Many years ago, I took a test related to profiles of CEOs. I discovered I was in the acceptable boundaries on only two out of twenty issues, and these were right in the margin. The psychologist suggested that, although I was succeeding as a CEO and probably would continue to do so, it was at a terrible cost to myself. I was forcing myself to do things that were destructive inside, but I didn't understand myself well enough to know that."

The third lesson was to search for a collaborative garden rather than a competitive one. That lesson from my garden is about symmetry and surprises. Symmetry in the garden has to do with harmonious proportions. Simply put, I've learned that I should stop getting carried away at the garden store and wanting one of everything.

When I put one of this and one of that next to each other, the result is competition instead of harmony. One plus one does not make two because they subtract from each other. When I make groupings of two's, three's or multiples of either, I get symmetry, harmony. Every plant seems to be enhanced by the others. They make a magnificent statement together. There is a time and place, however, for a surprise, a breaking of the rules, an innovation of heart and spirit.

The south side corner in the front of my house wanted to be noticed. It had all this great south and west sunlight and begged for something with height. It wanted one single trellis with a climbing plant. After a little research, I tried a Jackman Clematis. It was happy and climbing all over the place. It added a surprise velvet color behind the white Annabelle and a different height.

Another surprise solo is a spiral juniper tree in my raised stonewall garden corner. It, too, rises and unveils its green splendor in the unusual shape of a spiral staircase around the tree. The way these surprise solos collaborate is by drawing attention to the whole area around them, not just to themselves. The Solomon's Seal, Hosta, and Spirea all surround and hug the tree. Often, I add a pottery planter or hanging pouches with red impatiens. The red brings a splash of surprise as well as enhancing the greens.

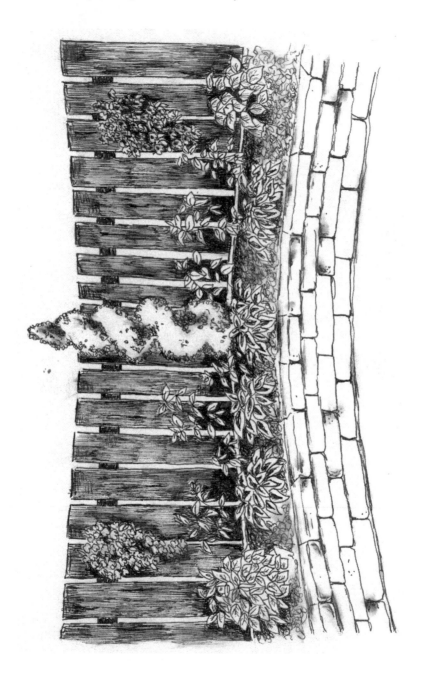

Room to Spare

Family life and home are the spaces within which we learn about belonging and togetherness or about separation and alienation. Belonging is a fundamental need beyond air, water, food, and shelter. A more important nourishment than food takes place when we gather together. That is the joy and warmth that comes from just being together, laughing, talking, sharing, and helping. Togetherness provides the knowledge that you belong, and that nourishes the heart, the spirit, and the relationships.

Some families draw a line around who may come to dinner. The definition of family is small and tight. They may be uncomfortable even including extended family or their children's friend, or a neighbor. Religion, race, or sexuality may also limit who is allowed. Other families may cast a very wide net including strangers from their church or a neighbor from down the block.

My Aunt Mary and Uncle Joe modeled how homes can expand in amazing ways when you want them to do so. No one else would have thought that they would have room to add me to the family, but they did. Elderly relatives were not forgotten at holidays. Someone always went to get the great aunt or uncle who lived alone.

Most people would not have been able to see how you could have weekend guests stay in that little house. When their college-age sons asked to bring classmates home for Thanksgiving or Easter because they were too far away from their own homes and had no where else to go, somehow our home expanded to accommodate them.

This was during the late 1950s and early 1960s. Some of those classmates were white East-coasters who the younger children thought had funny accents. Some were African American, Native American, or from other countries. There was always a place for them. There was never a single lecture or verbal comment; the actions spoke clearly and had a lasting impact. I don't pretend we were free from every prejudice, but we started on the path of inclusivity early in life. Those we bring into our homes become part of our "We." Those who never enter continue to be "Others." That lays the groundwork for harmony or separation, not just in a family, but also in a nation.

Aunt Mary could make food multiply and stretch a budget a long way. Uncle Joe could make a dining room grow. An extra piece of wood covered by a towel and hidden by a tablecloth made a lovely larger table with little expense. They expanded that table to include fifteen to twenty people. Everyone was seated in the dining room. Card tables supplemented the seating.

I put that experience into practice in my own way. We have about 850 square feet on our first floor and the dining room is about 12' x 12'. The table fits eight people if seen through the lens of "How big is the table?" My lens is "What can I change to serve food to all those I love?" My top number inside the house is about sixty if we have finger food. When weather allows us to expand to the yard in an open house format, we've managed a hundred-and-twenty-five. It just takes desire, creativity, and a willingness to move furniture and even put some of it in the basement or garage for a day. Space is for people, not things.

Expanding Your Home for the Day Rather than the Year

• Use coffee tables, end tables, card tables, and lap trays as well as the main table.

• Turn the dining room table at an angle and run a long folding table parallel to it doubling the number you can seat.

• Create many small eating areas in all the adjoining rooms, so people can cluster and talk.

• Serve finger food, so many people can stand and eat.

• Use the deck and yard to expand when possible.

• Make it an open house, so more can come and go as their schedules allow.

• Have gatherings that aren't based on full meals, so seating doesn't matter.

• Remove some furniture to the lower level or bedrooms to create more movement space, so people can mingle with a variety of groups.

Extended family can contribute to a wonderful sense of belonging and harmony, or they can also cause great friction. When you have two partners, then you confront the added potential impact of being torn between two families of origin. Differences in family sizes and traditions can also cause conflict. Harmony can triumph all these issues, if there is enough room to spare in hearts and minds.

Jan came from a large extended family. Jack was from a small, extended family all of whom lived out of town. Jan was an extrovert. Jack was somewhat introverted. Jack just could not understand why they had to attend every single birthday party, especially for the little kids, who wouldn't notice the difference if they were there or not. Nor did he see why they had to bend over backwards to have many gatherings in their home. For Jan, these events were fun and meaningful. For Jack, they were a lot less fun and interfered with his many athletic activities.

They struggled to find common ground. Both had strong feelings and a dozen arguments to support their case. When they were angry, insults flew about each other's families. They both began to dig their heels in deeper and deeper. When Jack did attend, he did it with an attitude. Jan began to dread looking at the calendar and seeing another family event approaching.

Jan talked to her brother, Sam, who offered a good insight. "Jack seems fine when he is talking with an adult or two. I think he is uncomfortable with the big group and the kids and how we mess around with them. I don't think he has any experience with kids. He'll change after he has kids of his own."

Later, though, Jan realized this issue needed to be settled before they had children. Sam's comments made her realize she hadn't been paying attention to Jack. She had only had room for her own desires and assumptions about how a family should be.

Eventually, they clarified their values, listened with open hearts to each other's stories about home and family, and used their creativity. Jack agreed that Jan could pick which events were her top priorities for him to attend. He would attend these willingly and warmly. Other events, Jan would attend without him. Sometimes he would come for a little while but could leave to join his friends in some athletic activity or just have downtime on his own. Jan helped her family come to understand that Jack's background was different, and his attendance or lack thereof had nothing to do with his affection for them.

Traditions give meaning and uniqueness to families, but they can become sources of stress, hurt feelings, and arguments. Traditions define doing things the right way based on how they have been done before. Meaning and harmony are about asking, what are the right things to do? and what matters most? Both are valuable and have their place. Traditions are created to pull people together, not to push them apart. When they are doing the latter, it is time for change.

Martha did not approve of one of her new daughters-in-law, Kathy. She criticized her career orientation and her lack of baking skills. When grandchildren came, Martha found much to be desired in how Kathy handled her children. Some of the criticisms were spoken, but most were indirect and subtle through body language. There was a common theme: "That's not how our family does it." Kathy was an inherently creative person, and that gift kept banging into a brick wall. Kathy's husband, Tom, was close to his family, and they were together frequently.

Tom didn't seem to notice the criticism or think it mattered. For Kathy, the hardest parts were feeling alone and being aware of the favoritism granted all the other grandchildren. Only one sister-in-law noticed and reached out. "You're not alone. Martha plays favorites with her own children. The boys rule and the girls come second. Tom has to deal with this, not you," she said. "The men in this family are accustomed to letting the women handle all these issues that you are struggling over with Mom. You need to help him see it. If he speaks up, she will listen."

Kathy was never able to get Tom to understand fully. He made some small attempts. She did begin to notice Martha's behavior toward her own daughters, so didn't feel singled out quite so much. Finally, she gave Martha one command, "Do not ever belittle me again in front of my children." No threat was issued, but Martha must have felt the firmness in her daughter-in-law, and grudgingly respected that. Kathy shifted the balance of interactions with Tom's family and concentrated more on her own family whose traditions celebrated her and welcomed Tom's differences.

Rituals and Rites of Passage
Anthropologists study universal phenomena that demonstrate what social hierarchies, values, and beliefs are important in specific cultures. Rites of passage are one of these phenomena. They are often ceremonies or rituals that a person must go through in order to progress to the next stage of their life. You might think of it as an experiential marker and learning experience at a turning point. Births, starting school, graduations, weddings, and funerals are significant events. How you start and end the day may be others. Perhaps you call a certain friend or family member every weekend. Anything can have a ritual to it, if we hold it as a sacred act.

The importance and visibility of significant events can

cast a shadow. Those days that are supposed to bring everyone together and reinforce loving bonds can become the source of anger, jealousy, and hurts that can mar relationships for a long time. Conflict develops over large and seemingly insignificant issues. Weddings are one of these that are particularly prone to these shadows as the bride, groom, and two or more parent groups try to navigate the waters.

At a time when harmony is a high value, there are many things to argue about: whom to invite, where to have the wedding, who will be in the wedding party, and how to deal with extended family with whom some members have had a rift. The costs of weddings add conflicts between parents and their adult children and between the bridal couple. The power of the purse can be used as a control mechanism, adding to the tension. All of these things become more intense as the size of the wedding increases.

Weddings have become more and more extravagant. In 2005, the average cost of a wedding had soared to $27,000. The average age of the wedding couple has also increased, and that has affected who pays for the wedding. Only a quarter of brides now expect their parents to pay for the whole wedding. About one-third of brides and grooms will pay for the total wedding.

Our daughter, Laura, became engaged the latter part of her sophomore year of college. She and her fiancé, Joe, had been friends since they were juniors in high school, so we understood that it seemed as if they had been waiting a long time. We encouraged them, however, to finish college first. They finally decided on August of the year following graduation.

Laura is an extremely organized person, so planning started early. They had many ideas ranging from the big traditional wedding to a small destination wedding. Some of that was curtailed when we reminded Laura of what we had told her a long time ago. She was responsible for paying for most of her wedding.

There were two reasons we had reached that conclusion. Our wedding story influenced us. We had made the decisions about our wedding and paid for it. It had been lovely, meaningful, and harmonious. We learned a great deal about each other from planning the service together. Negotiating the financial and priority setting aspects also set the stage for a lifetime of such activities. We wanted our daughter and future son-in-law to have similar opportunities.

This arrangement also helped to avoid arguments over the wedding. It belonged to her. If we were paying, though, I knew conflicts would be inevitable. We told her what we would contribute. From there, the boundaries and decision-making were clear. It also led to a great deal of values clarification on Laura and Joe's part about what their priorities were for the wedding.

There was a second reason. Bob's and my values are in conflict with the increased extravagance of weddings. We can respect someone else's preferences, but we weren't going to pay for it. After paying for private education, instruction in three musical instruments and orchestra, horseback-riding lessons, two travel abroad

J-terms in college, and more, we were reaching our limit. We would prefer to help with a down payment on a home when the time came than fund an extravagant wedding. So we turned the wedding over to Laura and Joe to steer and offered to support, participate, and walk with them any way they wanted. At least, we tried to do that most of the time.

Things started well. Laura and Joe put a budget together. Knowing it was largely their money had made an impact. Arrangements were made through church for the presider and guitarist whom we knew. Laura found the perfect wedding gown at a local consignment store for $325, much less than she had thought she would have to pay. It had never been worn, and it looked like it was made for her. Laura and Joe hired a photographer who took more casual friendly photos that matched their style rather than the traditional formal poses.

Joe's mother had been a florist at one time. She enlisted the help of another friend and agreed to teach Laura and one of her bridesmaids how to make bouquets. They would do all the flowers around our dining room table, have fun together, and save money. The flowers would be blessed with love.

We visited churches and alternative reception/event locations. Laura and Joe would get excited about one of them. Then the excitement would wane. Interestingly to me, they kept returning to, "We wish there was a way to have the wedding in the backyard" and, "We really want to get married outside." After this pattern repeated itself several times, their heart's desire was clear.

The problem was that none of us could figure out how to get enough people into our modest city lot or how to handle food. Laura has a large extended family. Joe's wasn't quite as large. We all had friends and neighbors to invite. Bob worried about an outdoor wedding, given potential weather issues, especially in hot August. We went back to looking at other facilities.

The bride and groom, however, continued to talk about how important our home was to both of them, especially to Laura. We were touched that all our efforts to create a meaningful home had affected her that deeply and that Joe felt similarly. Laura also acknowledged that her experience of the sacred was greater in nature than in a church. I had been hoping they would use our church or the beautiful chapel at Laura's college, so I had to let go of that wish.

The more we talked, it became clear that what mattered to them was a meaningful wedding service, at home, in the backyard, with an intimate grouping of the people with whom *they* had meaningful relationships, followed by a celebration with good food and conversation. The final pieces that mattered were to stay in a modest budget and have minimal stress. Their point about whom to invite was well taken. There are many relatives and friends with whom Bob or I have a relationship, but that Laura did not. We pared back the list, reluctantly. There still was not enough room.

Finally, I asked how they would feel about having two events. One could be the wedding with only the immediate family of sixty followed by a dinner at their favorite restaurant. Then we could have an open house reception several weeks later for extended family and friends. That opened the door to the best of both worlds—the intimate wedding and the inclusive celebration. They were enthusiastic about the idea and redid the budget.

As time passed more details became clear. The couple chose their favorite local Italian restaurant and rented a lovely room. They selected a family style service and foods that were family favorites. Then we dealt with Bob's concern about the weather. We would rent tents for the events in case of rain. If the weather was really bad, we could use the reception space for the wedding.

Eight months before the wedding, I had developed rheumatoid arthritis. I worried about the stress it would put on Laura, in particular, if I couldn't help with the coordination of so many wedding plans and the arrangements on the day itself.

I prayed I would improve. Gradually I did, although it was slow. In the meantime, two things happened that led to an insight about the stress of the wedding day. First, being ill had led me to think the day through in detail. Juggling to set up the rental chairs, the fabric in the yard, the centerpieces, and everything at the restaurant would be difficult. In addition, who would take everything down while we were at the reception?

Second, as I got better, I went to my friend BJ's birthday party. Her niece, Jamie, had done all the set up, and it was a lovely affair. Jamie had just graduated from college and wanted to start an event organizing business. I went home with Jamie's business card and gave it to Laura. We met with Jamie to discuss being a wedding coordinator. The girls hit it off. Jamie was excited to have the opportunity, and she gave us a reasonable proposal.

Laura liked the idea, but a wedding planner wasn't in the budget. Given my health constraints and the reasonableness of the cost, Bob and I agreed we would pay for that above and beyond the previous commitment. It was worth every penny. Jamie had good ideas, saved us money in other ways, and let all of us focus on enjoying what was meaningful.

The big day finally arrived. Our home seemed as joyful as we were. It and the garden wrapped their arms around the wedding party as we were graced with good weather. The backyard was transformed into a warm, elegant, sacred space, graced with draped fabric, greenery and flowers everywhere. Laura and Joe stood under our arbor as music and the carefully selected prayers filled the air.

Then the Presider spoke about Laura and Joe and how discerning they were about meaning, relationships, and the preparations that had gone into creating this moment. Tears came to my eyes as he talked about the love that had consecrated this ground, making it holy. He quoted the Irish blessing that had just been read, "May the wind always be at your back. May the sun shine warm upon your face." He said it seemed to speak of the breeze we were feeling and sun shining on us but also the people who were carefully chosen to be here. They were the lasting wind and sun at Laura and Joe's backs.

Many guests told us that this was the most beautiful and intimate wedding they had attended. Something

about being in our home, having the smaller group that allowed Joe and Laura to mingle without stress, and having such a thoughtful and personal service touched them. And later, everyone loved the food at the restaurant.

As I looked at the wedding pictures afterward, I was struck by all the years of effort that had gone into creating a meaningful and harmonious home. The images that looked back at me were fulfilling and affirming. We certainly had no idea that a wedding and uniting of families would take place here, but our home and yard looked as though they had dressed for the occasion.

Home, Work, and Electronics

It has taken many centuries to separate work from home, but that trend is being reversed in recent decades. There are three main causes. There has been a significant increase in self-employment with individuals who operate from their homes. About 5.7 million Americans worked at home in 2008, up from 4.2 million in 2000. There is even an emerging market for a new type of housing called live/work housing. Condo or apartment units may have two doors—one to the street and one to the apartment allowing easy separation of the living part from the business part.

A second factor has been the rise in the number of organizations that are allowing their employees to work from home full or part-time. A third factor that is now affecting almost everyone—the employed, unemployed, and self-employed—is the arrival of electronic devices that, if allowed, keep us connected to work 24/7.

For some people, these trends have led to greater harmony and more time at home. For others, it feels more like an invasion even at the dinner table and in the bedroom. For some it is the new addiction. There is proof all around us that humans are not always effective at acting on warning signs.

Despite evidence that texting is spawning a new physical ailment; we buy more devices and use them more. I thought it was a joke the first time I heard of Blackberry

Thumb. Then I saw articles about it. In one, Margot Miller, President of the American Physical Therapy Association's Occupational Health Special Interest Group, stated, "Because the keyboard of the PDA is so small, and because the thumb, which is the least dexterous part of the hand, is overtaxed, the risk of injury just skyrockets." If we do not heed physical evidence, we are even less likely to take note of challenges to less tangible things like home and harmony.

One evening Chris sat in her family room watching her husband and children. They had invested in the new addition the previous year. They had expanded and revamped the kitchen and opened it up to the new space that was to be the family room. The whole idea was to give them a more integrated space so that they could spend more time together as they cooked, ate, talked, did homework, and read the paper, as well as watch TV as a family.

John, her husband, was engrossed working on his laptop. Charlie, their ten-year-old, had to ask his dad three times if he was coming to the soccer game on Friday. Once that was settled, he returned to his Game Boy. Jenny, their fifteen-year-old, was watching television, doing homework, and texting at the same time. Many evenings, Chris would also spend some time on the computer after dinner, checking emails, both work and family related.

An hour ago, when Chris had announced dinner and told everyone to turn their devices off, there had been complaints. When she made it clear that the television was to be turned off as well, even John objected saying he wanted to hear the news. This was not the picture that they had in mind when they agreed to create the family room. Talking to her mother later that evening she said, "All we have accomplished is physical co-location. The family room isn't functioning as a family room. It's really a television and electronic device center."

Jenny was a nurse. Her husband, Fred, had his business office in their home. She became increasingly concerned and angry when Fred started keeping his cell phone on at night under his pillow. She would hear him getting up and down in the middle of the night if there were urgent calls from his business partners in China. She complained to friends that the cell phone had become a permanent appendage.

Karol, Sandy, and Rob formed their own support group. They were all self-employed and had met at a networking breakfast. They discovered they all were fighting the same battle, and it wasn't with business competitors. The battle was internal. They had all been partly motivated to start their own businesses so they could have more balance in life and time at home, yet they found that their home offices were starting to take over their whole lives and homes. Rob summed it up, "The office seems to have tentacles and no matter where I go in the house or what I do, it reaches out and grabs me."

In 1989, I joined the ranks of the self-employed by starting my own consulting business. I interviewed other people who were self-employed before I made my decision of how and where to start my business. One of the most significant insights I received was to be exceedingly careful about managing my boundaries between home and work.

I was warned about the potential distractions of laundry, children, and the yard. Others talked about gaining weight from raiding the refrigerator too easily. Some were lonely.

One person recommended that I needed to rise with the alarm clock every day, shower and dress for the office, pick up my briefcase, and walk down the hall to the office, and keep the door shut all day unless leaving to see a client. On the other hand, some described how great it was to stay in your jeans, if you weren't seeing clients. They loved the freedom of arranging their day any way they wanted to accommodate client deadlines and their own desires. They had boundaries defined by goals, deadlines, and priorities. They were less distinct boundaries guided by values, not the clock. I decided to be like them.

I worked my way through the challenges and distractions. The greatest challenge today is the 24/7 expectations. I have my own guidelines that work for me. They help me draw boundaries and maintain them in a non-offensive manner.

My Boundary Guidelines

• Say "no" to work for which I am not qualified or when I have any reservations about the client.

• Keep office hours of 8:30 am–5:30 PM. (I can work other hours but at my choice, not as part of normal expectations.)

• Have an office phone number separate from my home number and turn off the ringer beyond office hours.

• Limit how many people have my cell phone number.

• Turn the cell phone off according to office hours.

• Seldom do I give out a home number for business purposes.

• Do not allow the cell phone to interrupt a meaningful discussion.

vHave limited involvement with any form of social media that is unproductive.

• Plan my day based on desired outcomes and promises made.*

• Stay abreast of many methodologies, so I never become the kind of consultant my clients call the "hammer and nail" consultant.**

Exceptions are allowed to most of these rules, but on a case-by-case basis, rather than with a frequency that means the rules disappear.

*If I have a deadline for a client, then no home distractions are allowed. If I have time and want to enjoy a lovely sunny afternoon, then do it guilt-free.

** What they mean is that the consultant has one tool (a hammer). The tool is the same solution to every problem because every problem looks like a nail to the consultant.

I don't offer these as the right rules for someone else. I offer them as an example of the kind of thinking process you may want to consider if you want harmony and a meaningful home to include your workplace. My rules are driven by my values, personality, and relationship to money.

Food for Thought

• Lectures are so tempting but likely to fail. They just make the others angry or defensive.

• Pleasure is a strong attractor so try to use that instead to encourage family members to rethink behavior.

• Karol, Sandy, and Rob have the right idea. Find others who are dealing with the same issues.

• According to Aristotle: "We are what we repeatedly do. Excellence, then, is not an act, but a habit." Work on new habits and be creative about them.

• Children do need to be told "no" at times and have good role models.

• Start with changing your own behavior before you ask others to change theirs. Your integrity must show through if you want to influence someone else.

There is a story about Gandhi that illustrates this. A woman came to him seeking help with stopping her child from eating too much sugar that exacerbated his health issues. Gandhi sent her and her child away for a period of time after which they were to return.

When they did return, Gandhi looked at the child and with great seriousness told the child that his life depended on stopping the habit of eating sugar. The mother asked him, "Why didn't you just tell him that the first time we were here?" Gandhi replied, "First, I had to stop eating sugar myself."

~

Reflections/Suggestions for Another Day:

• Describe what communication patterns help restore harmony in your home.

• How does your furniture and its arrangement contribute to unity and harmony?

• What life lessons have you learned from gardening?

• What areas in your life are examples of where your expectations for others or your home do not fit the soil that is available?

• What rituals and rites of passage have you experienced in your home and how harmonious were they? Could you do something different next time?

• What are your greatest challenges with work and home boundaries that you intend to shift?

• Review pages 229–230 about *Messages From Water.* What kind of crystal formation would be created by the sounds of your home?

• Consider having a dialog about the use of electronics in your home.

• If you have times when you want to expand your space, try the previous suggestions.

Leaving Home

Joseph Campbell and others have written about the hero's journey. The hero or heroine leaves the everyday world to enter the unknown where challenging forces are encountered, and a victory is won. The hero returns with gifts for humanity. In my book, the heroic journey is about taking the risks to love with all your might. Building a home and a life conceived in love for family and neighbor ensures you will have joy and pain—the pain of loss. As Gibran says, "When you are joyous, look deep into your heart and you shall find it is only that which has given you sorrow that is giving you joy."

The more you have consciously chosen to know thyself; create a life of goodness, truth and beauty; live according to nothing in excess; and devote your life not just to family, but to the global community, the more you have been on the hero's journey. You have been creating a meaningful home, work, and life that contribute to others beyond your lifetime.

There are daily acts that look the same on the outside but are different on the inside. We all begin with the normal expectations of whatever our culture decrees. We may move out of our parents' home to one of our own. We may marry and have children. We may choose the single life. We may become a homeowner. The degree of intention and thoughtfulness in those actions and commitment to a higher sacredness makes all the difference between what Campbell may have called the "way of the common life" and the "way of the hero." Something in the life of the hero or heroine calls him or her to the adventure of the "examined life."

There are challenges and temptations in this journey. For one hero, providing safety and the basic necessities may be the challenge. For other modern heroes, the ego is a great temptation. Will the hero/heroine build a home or a showcase house? Both will love their children, but one will offer a home of unconditional love, the discipline to say "no," and the encouragement to be compassionate. The other will give their child all the means to perform well, offer support for a 24/7 life style, and will revel in the child's accomplishments.

The journey will have an end. The heroic live with that consciousness and use it to inspire. Others choose to not think about it. Some of them will still live a good life. Others will live for the day and for themselves. They have a right to choose, unless they hurt others.

There are many new resources for people through all the stages of your journey. You may want to explore what is available in your area. One group that I am familiar with is called Third Act Life Discovery (www.thirdact-ministry.org). The leaders ask you to consider the question, "For your third act in life, who will you be and how do you want to live?" One of their offerings is a Spiritual Home Makeover.

Homeless

Some people live their entire lives in the same home; others have had many places they have called home. Doris has had twenty-three homes over a period of twenty-four years as her husband drifted from one school or job to another. She had to divorce him before she could become rooted in a home. Life circumstances may force individuals to leave homes they love. Then again, some can't wait to leave a childhood home and create their own. Later in life, some adults choose to stay in their homes as long as possible, while others are ready to downsize and start a new adventure.

A friend's story took me to an understanding of home that is fundamental. At first my questions were focused on her unique experience. How do you build a home for yourself in the world, if you have never had a safe and loving home? It is hard to lose your home, but what if you never had one? The more I thought about her experience, a common thread emerged that relates to all of us. Regardless of our choices or circumstances in life, ultimately, we all build our homes in the physical world starting with the way we live in our interior world.

By the time I met Terrie, she was a successful businessperson with a Master's degree in Human Development.

No one would have guessed how differently she had lived earlier in life. As with all profound stories, it is hard to decide where to start. The first glimpse I had of her life happened this way.

Terrie was involved in a variety of activities for the homeless. One night over dinner, she told me why they mattered so much to her. She had been in their shoes when she was young, she confided. She had lived in a white '68 Chevy Impala Super Sport with her sixteen-month-old baby girl for months while she earned enough money to drive from New Mexico to her old home in Minnesota. She gave me permission to tell her story from her soon to-be-released book entitled *Move*.

Just as she was turning seventeen, she discovered she was pregnant. Giving the baby away wasn't an option for her, so she chose marriage. Both sets of parents witnessed the marriage, ensuring the young couple followed through with the plan to save face with their church and community. Terrie was aware of only one incident of divorce in her life. Trusting in several fairy tales with happy endings, she believed things would be fine.

Soon after the wedding, she found herself in a military town in Colorado nine hundred miles away from home, alone and wounded. Her body was bruised. Her husband began abusing her on the day they were married and that continued. She gave birth to her daughter and hoped that things would change.

They did change, but for the worse. By the time the military transferred them to New Mexico, the daily fear she lived in deepened. She never knew what would set him off and cause him to strike her. After many hospital stays, she was served divorce papers. He was divorcing her after their brief marriage on grounds that she had deserted him due to her hospital stays.

She said that the courtroom scene could have been made for the movies. She was nearly nineteen-years-old as she sat bruised and shaken on the witness stand. The aging judge asked her if the man standing before him in front of the bench was the one who caused her injuries. Almost inaudibly, she whispered, "Yes."

With a smash of his gavel, he declared, "Divorce granted." She had to be helped down from the stand, hobbling from a cracked tailbone, and unable to see through her blinding tears of relief.

She was awarded her husband's prized Impala Super Sport. That was a good thing, as it would become her home for a while. She chose the car as her safest alternative, given she didn't have money to rent a place. The car became a welcomed sanctuary for the rest of her time in New Mexico. She spoke of the car almost tenderly. She described its supple red leather interior. I could almost see the sixteen-month-old baby girl sleeping on a cotton duck print blanket on the seat in the back.

Terrie went on to describe how few resources there were for young women in the 1970s and how clueless she was about almost everything. Despite that, she was incredibly grateful for several things—a job, childcare, a safe place to park, and a place to use a bathroom and shower.

She found a job waitressing. Another waitress offered the parking space outside of her home, and the use of her bathroom and shower on days when her roommate was traveling. Conveniently, the sheriff lived on the left side of the street where she parked her car. He would check on her now and then to ensure things were fine. He and his wife always left their outside light on at night making her feel safe, like someone was watching over her and her child.

When we were discussing my book and her story, I said it sounded like the car was more than a car, that it really was a home. "Yes," she said, "home is where you are safe. Living in a safe car was so much better than a violent house." She reflected on her journey and what she had learned. There was a long pattern of abuse starting in her childhood.

She doesn't think she even felt safe in the womb and didn't know how to inhabit her own body because it was so fearful. She kept returning to her theme of home as a physically and emotionally safe place. Beautiful houses that were physically safe, but not emotionally safe, weren't really homes. They were less of a home than the car because the car was emotionally safe. Finding that safe haven lets you begin to take a step forward. She said, "Homelessness is partly a state of mind. The good news is you can change your mind."

One night, during Terrie's stay in the Impala, she was leaning against the steering wheel, staring up at the stars. In a moment of clarity that came from somewhere in her body, she felt—and stated out loud—with a powerful sense of conviction that she would someday start her own business and drive a Jaguar. She thought they were the most beautiful cars on the road—sleek, sexy, and sassy. Owning a business would afford her financial freedom.

After a long haul, Terrie owns her business and is financially sound and free. She also has made a home in the world for herself and her child against the odds, but not without scars. That Impala gave her the safe space to create a vision of a new life. She fulfilled her vision, developed a flourishing business, and leased a Jaguar for two years. She said, "I didn't do it out of ego. I needed to make that dream come true for a sense of accomplishment. I wanted to be able to look back at that young girl in the Impala in the desert and tell her that she did it!"

Terrie had this experience when there were fewer institutional resources available than today, but she was fortunate to find individuals who befriended her. They were people with limited financial resources of their own but with rich hearts. If we look at the number of homeless people today, despite more institutional resources, it does make me wonder what our society wants to be. You can also feel homeless, even when you have a house. How does early home life affect us for the rest of our adult lives? Here are things I wonder:

• If I am a child who is lacking in house, will I seek a way to get food and shelter by theft, begging, or whatever means I can find, including invading your home?

• If I am a child who is lacking in loving and present parents, I may also seek some other form of parent or make my own tribe. That could be a healthy adult like a grandparent or an unhealthy adult like a pimp. I may find a home of sorts in a gang, an athletic team, or a sexual relationship.

• Perhaps I am a child rich in all the elements of house but poor in the home dimensions; I may be an overachiever with or without ethics as a means to earn a sense of home. I may turn to drugs or sex as a way to fill the void.

• As an adult, I may turn to food to try to fill either or both of these voids and struggle with my weight. Or, I may have learned that the warmth of home was closely bound with food so it brings me comfort in this frantic world.

• As an adult, I may have a work pattern of over-achieving, feeling that recognition, money, and power will fill one or both of these voids.

• What do you wonder?

Foreclosure Heartbreak
PPeople lose their homes for different reasons, and they process how they lose their homes in diverse ways. In the last few years our country has been faced with a massive mess from foreclosures that is heartbreaking. Many of these people were victims of fraud. We have friends who were among the first wave of the fraud cases. The timing is sad. If they were in trouble now, there are new tools available to help people, and they probably would not have lost their home.

Alice began the story. "We were married at a young age, and it was fifteen years before we could afford a house. We drove around looking at houses and dreaming. We often wondered if those owners really knew how lucky they were. Finally, we were ready to buy a house. We have relatives in the real estate business who were helping us. They took me to see a house early in the day before Dave was available, and I didn't like it, but I knew Dave would love it."

Dave continued. "I saw it that night. Where Alice saw a house in sad shape I saw tons of potential. It was selling for $89,000 in 1997 and that was pretty cheap. Alice wanted a story-and-a-half house, and this was a three-bedroom rambler. It was in a good neighborhood with good schools. I argued we should go for it before someone else snatched it up."

Alice smiled and said, "We made something out of nothing. People came over all the time and didn't want to leave. They loved our home. It felt very safe, and it was beautiful. Our house changed our whole neighborhood. People would come over and thank us for moving in. The boys always had friends over—usually the whole hockey team that Dave coached. Our home had the kind of warmth you can't buy. It's the feeling you have if you are sick, and someone gently puts a blanket over your shoulders that is right out of the dryer and wraps it around your feet. I miss it so."

Dave took up the story. "We ended up having to sell the house ten years to the day we bought it on Alice's birthday. We sold for about $279,000, but we walked away, not only without any profit, but even had to pay some money. Our work had tripled the value of the house, but we never got any of that.

"Prior to this we had refinanced a couple of times to pay for the roof, a garage, and other improvements. We had paid those off. Then we wanted to take out a small equity loan for the kids' schooling and to pay off about

$11,000. We got a referral from a reliable source for a company that they did not know well. The new broker kept pushing us to refinance the whole house rather than the small amount we wanted. They said we would get more cash and get a lower mortgage payment. We felt something was wrong, but we got caught. We contacted the attorney general's office.

"We were struggling and the situation went from bad to worse. When the attorney general's office was ready to start proceedings, the broker company dissolved itself. Our mortgage payments were going to a P.O. box. At one point we had to send about $30,000 through Western Union. It disappeared, and we didn't have the resources to do anything about it.

"We thought we were going to walk away with at least $15–20,000 if we could sell the house. We sold it one day before the sheriff's sale was to occur, and we ended up having to pay $8000 after all was said and done. The fraudulent lender had disappeared after ruining our credit and reputation.

"I think this has been harder on Alice than me, although I have also been depressed. Alice wanted to fight, but I got to the point that I just wanted to move on. The meanness of the whole thing just nauseated me. I've probably moved fourteen times in my life, so moving again wasn't as big an issue."

"I did want to keep fighting," Alice said. "I had lived in one home my whole life until we got married. My dad was an immigrant and had worked hard to achieve home ownership. When he died he wanted to know that Dave,

I, and the boys were going to be all right. I felt like losing the house was somehow not living up to his expectations. I wanted my children to have a permanent home. For me that is stability.

"I really miss so many things. Dave had built-in so much of the furniture, so we had to buy a lot of things such as night stands and dressers. Only the bed came with us from the bedroom. I really miss my garden and sitting on the front steps watching Dave mow the grass and having neighbors stop to chat."

Dave added, "I miss things, too. I like to be active. I miss mowing the lawn and even snow blowing. My grandparents had a family farm in North Dakota. I had hauled that rich soil down as well as family potatoes to start my own potato patch."

"I think we are still grieving," Alice commented. "I don't like not knowing for sure where we will be in a year. I don't like not owning because then I can do what I want with my space. I feel embarrassed, ashamed, and as if I have been eating humble pie because of the whole situation. We were naïve about the meanness. There really are some bad people in the world. I don't know how they live with themselves. I feel shame that we let people do that to us. At least we were able to testify at the legislature on a bill to deal with this issue. We wanted to try to help others not get caught like we did.

"We have each other and our health. We still have our children, who are grown and on their own. We brought a lot of meaningful things from the house. I haven't even been able to unpack all of them. Dave has invested his skill and time in the condo that we rent and that has made a difference. It does feel like home, especially when the kids come over.

"At times I do the, 'Why me?' We cared for my parents, we worked hard to get a house, we tried to give the boys security, and I feel like it isn't fair. In the end, I know that we have to go on for the people we care about. Our one son has a wonderful two-year-old and we love spending time with her. Our other son and daughter-in-law bought a home last year. I have the time to help them with their yard and Dave has saved them a great deal of money repairing things in the house. He enjoys teaching them what he has learned. Right now, it's hard to see beyond where we are, but we trust we will make it."

The Last Leaving

FFor many of us, our pets teach us about death. Children learn many things from pets including responsibility and giving, not just receiving. The hardest lesson is about letting go. Our dog, Athena, began to have seizures and died. It all happened so fast, the vet hadn't even figured out what was wrong. In that short time, Laura overcame her fear of the seizures and wanted to help comfort her puppy. She would sit and stroke her and whisper, "It's OK. It's OK."

When Athena died, it was Laura's first experience with death. It was heartbreaking for all of us, especially for me, since Athena helped make my apartment my home. With their shorter life spans, our pets help us to experience loss, grief, and healing before we lose the precious people in our lives.

When most people lived on farms, they had a lifetime of experience with illness, dying, and death. In today's city-based living and given modern medicine's patterns, we are more removed from this natural but difficult process. While there are benefits to this, there are also disadvantages. Perhaps when we finally confront death, we are less well equipped than previous generations. If we have lost pets, they can help create a bridge when age or illness forces us to leave home or to die.

If we live long enough, we have learned to let go of those we love as our parents, spouses, siblings, and friends die. We make choices about staying in our homes, downsizing, moving into assisted living, or other options. How we feel about our homes affects those choices.

I have childhood memories of going to Aunt Pearl and Uncle Lawrence's home for holidays and playing with my many cousins. My uncle died years ago, but Aunt Pearl, at the age of ninety-six, was still living alone in her home of sixty years. Visiting her home was like stepping back in time to the 1960s and 1970s relative to furnishings and decorating. What was important was that she liked what she had, took loving care of it, and it was filled with memories. She was proud of her home and felt secure in it.

Her neighborhood meant a great deal to her. She had a wonderful relationship with her neighbors. They frequently invited her to baptisms, confirmations, and other family events. They were good to her in other ways, offering help when her children couldn't come over. The neighborhood also contributed to her sense of safety. All that love and support made a significant difference in allowing her to stay in her home.

She had a special friend, Bill, who was also very active and helpful, and she had a dear sister. Aunt Pearl had become a teacher in her forties after her youngest son reached school age, so she still had many teacher friends who were younger than she was. She socialized with these teachers, her sister, and other friends. She loved to have them come for lunch. Her home was a center for a rich and active life.

Aunt Pearl was one of the most sociable people I have ever met. She loved people and conversation. Even when she would travel, people and conversations were the priority. When almost anyone else would be reporting on the sights they had seen and things they had done, Aunt Pearl would describe the interesting people she had met on the bus. Every time I saw her at a wedding, funeral, family reunion, or any other event, she would hold tight to my arm, look up into my eyes, and say, "Oh, do come see me."

The last time I responded to her invitation was in the winter before she moved into an assisted living apartment. When I called to say I was coming over, she was thrilled and wanted to make lunch for me. I didn't want to burden her. Finally, we compromised. I would bring lunch, and she would provide dessert.

We had a pleasant lunch, and then she brought out dessert. She had made, not one, but three kinds of cookies for me. The plate was loaded. She talked about how she loved to bake and said she did so almost every day. Her kitchen was a favorite room. Considering that I make cookies about once a year, I just could not comprehend that idea and had no idea who ate all of them. I asked one of my cousins about it. He said the neighbors got cookies all the time. Often it was the children, but sometimes the adults received them as well. Food was love in her mind. It was her way of expressing affection, concern, and gratitude; it could also provide an excuse to interact.

After dessert, she wanted to walk around her home and show me things that meant a great deal to her. She touched things with such love. While she didn't see well any more, nor hear that well, it didn't matter. She had the house memorized. Then we went through eight picture albums and ninety years of memories. The memories were as sweet and filling as the cookies. Some were more bittersweet. It was starting to get dark by the time I left. It could be difficult to get away from Aunt Pearl. It was wonderful, and I vowed to make my visits more frequent.

When I heard that she was moving into assisted living, I was relieved but sad. She had taken a fall a number of years before this; she always thought she could manage steps and things that other people thought she should not do. Winters were hard on her because she couldn't be outside and see all the neighborhood activity. She was becoming fearful at night. I could only imagine how difficult moving from her home was going to be for her and hoped it would go well. They had found a lovely assisted living apartment only five minutes from one of her sons.

She struggled with the move. She missed her home and all her neighbors and friends. She cried quite a bit and had no interest in cooking in her new little kitchen. Despite visits by her children, grandchildren, and great grandchildren, she complained of being lonely with no one around. I wonder if she really meant without her "home" around her. One of the other residents at the facility made a special effort to become friends. That made a difference until another change came.

After a bout of pneumonia, she needed more care and could not move back to her apartment. The only unit that was available to provide the necessary support was the memory care unit, even though her memory was fine. My cousins believe that she wasn't getting enough daily stimulation, and she lost interest in eating and participating in activities. The last few times I saw her, she sounded lost, unhappy, and confused. She died at the age of ninety-eight.

Many of us hope to leave a legacy. The home she and my uncle created touched four children and their spouses, thirteen grandchildren, twenty-two great grandchildren, one great-greatgrandchild and an abundance of nieces, nephews, friends, neighbors, and former students. Aunt Pearl's former home goes on living. After some refurbishment, it is now providing a home to another family.

People often speak of how lost they feel after a death of a loved one, after a move from their home, or the loss of a job. A friend and I were talking about the recent death of her mother. My friend, too, felt "lost." She made an insightful comment about losing mothers. "You know, my mom's body was my first home in this world. I've lost my first home."

I keep thinking about that. Perhaps our mothers hold us in, protect us, and shelter us. I thought about fathers as well. And for me, my father's arms were my second home in the world. They supported me and helped me stretch out to the world, whether it was reaching for the swing-set high bar or a paintbrush. Maybe mothers provide safe havens and fathers encourage reaching into the world. I wonder, "Is part of our need for a physical home to help ease the loss that has already come, or we know one day will come as we lose our parents? Is losing a home an emotional experience of losing love and a haven?"

The most common meaning of "lost" is not being able to find something. What else does "lost" really mean? I found all the following definitions for lost:

• No longer in your possession or control; unable to be found or recovered

  • Incapable of being recovered or regained
  • Spiritually or physically doomed or destroyed
  • Confused: having lost your bearings
  • Confused: as to time or place or personal identity
  • Bemused: deeply absorbed in thought
• Baffled: perplexed by many conflicting situations or statements; filled with bewilderment
  • Doomed: people who are destined to die soon
  • Helpless: unable to function without help

Suggestions When Feeling Lost
• Make a small haven somewhere both inside of you and around you.
  • Do simple acts of beauty.

• Expect help, so that you see it when it shows up.

• Don't be too strong to ask for and use help.

• Explore what the intangible loss is associated with the physical loss. Rebuild both.

• Look to see if there is someone else you can comfort.

• Be comforted, knowing that "home" is always inside of you waiting to be drawn out.

• Leave a trail of crumbs (memories and good deeds) to follow.

Perhaps home teaches about attachment and letting go. It helps us become more attached to people, pets, plants, trees, grass, and all nature. Home also attaches us to things and what they represent whether that is comfort or prestige, beauty or recognition, and giving or receiving. We become attached to values and learn what has value to us.

The difficult lesson of letting go will come. Our children will grow and leave us for homes of their own. Pets and plants will die. We will grow older and our bodies will change, despite all our efforts to the contrary. We may need to leave the house we called home and many possessions. In the end, we, too, will have to let go of all we hold dear, even the body that is our physical home. If we are fortunate, we will leave a legacy that matters and lives through others. May we leave our final home with grace. A home that has been conceived in love and beauty significantly contributes to the meaning of our living and leaving as we say "Goodbye."

I don't mean just the big final "Goodbye." I also mean the daily goodbyes. What will we take from our homes out into the world each day? Will the world be a little better place because of what our homes have done for us? We need government, non-profits, schools, and businesses to help solve a host of challenges from health to climate change, from energy resources to loneliness, to the future of the next generation. None of these institutions can solve the problems without healthy, happy, harmonious homes that inspire their members to take responsibility for creating a good life for themselves and their neighbors; home is where it all starts and ultimately ends.

~

Reflections/Suggestions for Another Day:

• What have been the challenges and teachings from your heroic journey so far?

• When have you felt homeless, whether you had a home or not? What did you learn?

• How did that feel?

• How did you find your way home?

• If you were to do a reckoning of the home you have built, how satisfied would you be?

• What new elements do you want to create after reading this book?

• What would it take for you to commit to doing that?

• How would you hang on to hope if you were ever in Terrie's or Dave and Alice's shoes?

• If you had to leave your home, what would you miss the most?

• What legacy do you want to leave?

Dreams to Reality

Not much happens without a dream.
And for something great to happen,
there must be a great dream.
Behind every great achievement
is a dreamer of great dreams.
Much more than a dreamer
is required to bring it to reality,
but the dream must be there first.

Robert K. Greenleaf
The Servant as Leader

To further support your dreams, please see the following pages for references to other books, as well as my services, and a sample excerpt of a recommended book.

My dream is for this book to help thousands of people create happier homes, but I can't do that alone. Please consider recommending it to others through conversations, social media, blogging, emails, writing a review on Amazon.com or giving it as a gift. See my website (lulic-books.com) for materials or sign up for a newsletter that you can use and forward to friends.

In gratitude,
Margaret Lulic

Recommended Books and Articles

Books

Barnes, Peter. *Who Owns the Sky?* (Island), 2001

Bopp, Julia. Bopp, Michael. Brown, Lee. Lane, Phil. *The Sacred Tree* (Lotus Light), 1984

de Botton, Alain. *The Architecture of Happiness* (Vintage), 2008

Buettner, Dan. *The Blue Zones, Lessons for Living Longer From the People Who've Lived The Longest* (National Geographic), 2008

Busch, Akiko. *Geography of Home* (Princeton Architectural Press), 1999

Cooper Marcus, Clare. *House as a Mirror of Self* (Conari), 1995

Csíkszentmihályi, Mihály. *Flow: The Psychology of Optimal Experience* (Rider), 2002

Emoto, Masaru. *The Hidden Messages in Water* (Beyond Words), 2001

Ferrucci, Pierro. *Beauty and the Soul* (Tarcher/Penguin), 2009

Gallagher, Winifred. *House Thinking* (Harper), 2006

Gibran, Kahlil. *The Prophet* (New York: Knopf), 1968

Hawken, Paul. *The Magic of Findhorn* (New York: Harper), 1975

Hyder, Carole. *Conversations with Your Home, Guidance and Inspiration beyond Feng Shui* (Minneapolis: Hyder Enterprises), 2010

Lulic, Margaret. *Who We Could Be at Work* (Butterworth Heinnemann), 1994

Morrow Lindbergh, Anne. *Gift from the Sea* (Pantheon), 1955

Morris, Tom. *If Aristotle Ran General Motors* (New York: Henry Holt), 1997

Naisbitt, John. *Megatrends: Ten New Directions Transforming Our Lives* (Warner), 1982

Putman, Robert. *Bowling Alone, The Collapse and Revival of American Community* (New York: Simon and Schuster), 2001

Suransky Polakow, Valerie. *The Erosion of Childhood* (Chicago: University of Chicago), 1982

Rath, Tom. Harter, James K. Ph.D. *Wellbeing: The Five Essential Elements* (Deckle Edge), 2010

Ray, Paul. Anderson, Sherry. *The Cultural Creatives: How 50 Million People Are Changing the World* (Harmony), 2000

Remen, Rachel Naomi. *Kitchen Table Wisdom: Stories That Heal* (New York: Riverhead), 1996

Rosenberg, Marshall. *Nonviolent Communication: A Language of Life* (PuddleDancer Press), 2003

Rybczynski, Witold. *Home: A Short History of An Idea* (Penguin), 1986

Schor, Juliet. *The Overworked American* (BasicBooks), 1992

Sheldrake, Rupert. *Dogs that Know When Their Owners Are Coming Home* (Three Rivers), 1999

Stuart, David E. *Anasazi America* (University of New Mexico), 2000

Susanka, Sarah. *The Not So Big House* (Tauton), 1998

Swimme, Brian. *The Universe is A Green Dragon: A Cosmic Creation Story* (Bear), 2001

Ten Eyck, Terrie. *Move.* unpublished at this time

Tuan, Professor Yi-Fu. *Letter Dear Colleague* 2009

Articles, Documents and Web sites

Berland, Michael. 2010. Compassion Counts More Than Ever. *Parade Magazine*

Gibbs, Nancy. 2006. The Magic of the Family Meal. *Time*

Ginsburg, Kenneth R. MD. 2007. The Importance of Play in Promoting the Healthy Development of Children and Maintaining Strong Parent-Child Bonds. *American Academy of Pediatrics.*

Hill, Tyler. 2008. Three Charity Sites That Let Donors Call the Shots. *SmartMoney*

Kuo, Francis. 2009. Science Suggests that Access to Nature is Essential to Human Health. *ScienceDaily*

American Society for Horticultural Science. 2008. (ASHS Press Release). The Perfect Gift for Hospital Patients.

Anxiety Disorders Association of America. 2006 Stress & Anxiety Disorders Survey.

http://www.womenwork.org/pdfresources/StressOutWeekpress-release.pdf

Convention on the Rights of the Child General Assembly Resolution 44/25 of 20 November 1989. Accessed June 22, 2006. J Educ Psychol. 1999; 91:76–97.

http://www.unhchr.ch/html/menu3/b/k2crc.htm

Service Options for You

If you want assistance with creating a *Home—Inspired by Love and Beauty,* I'd love to help you. I coach, speak, and conduct workshops. Here's what others have experienced:

"I couldn't have become the author I am today without the help Margaret gave me. With her adept counsel, I learned I could do things I hadn't thought possible."
  —Sarah Susanka, Author, *The Not So Big House*

"Margaret thinks out of the box and is capable of leading others out of their boxes. A born philosopher, she draws wisdom out of others."
  —Charles M. Denny, retired CEO
    ADC Telecommunications, Inc.

"Approaching 70 years of age, I wanted to optimize my future years. I hired a Life Coach. Within two sessions, I felt as if Margaret had known me forever. Her questions led me to discover my own wisdom, vision, and to develop an action plan. Margaret is safe, nonjudgmental, and professional. Her guidance has far exceeded my expectations."
  —Sue Davern, Happier person, wife, mother, and
    grandmother

"We were struggling with making expensive investments to our duplex including issues of windows and color. What we had hoped to be exciting was becoming a conflict. In an amazingly short amount of time, Margaret helped us define a process that restored harmony and collaboration."
  —Two Happy Homeowners

For more information go to www.lulicbooks.com
To make an appointment for a session—in-person or by telephone—
call 612-920-0637 or email Margaret@lulicbooks.com

Don't Stop Now!

If you appreciated my book consider the following:

Read *Conversations with Your Home, Guidance and Inspiration beyond Feng Shui* by Carole J. Hyder, M.A. In this intriguing and original approach you will learn to create a new relationship with your home. Hyder teaches you how to receive answers from your shelter about who you really are and were meant to be, and what you and your space could create together to bring you more health, beauty, and happiness. Archetypes, exercises, and stories will show you the way. Brilliant!

Carole and I have been writing partners for these two wonderful books drawing on each other for wisdom, inspiration, and support so that they may serve you with the best information and insights from a diverse world of experience.

Read on for a small taste of her book.
Available through carolehyder.com and amazon.com

Excerpt from *Conversations with Your Home*
by Carole J. Hyder, M.A.

> My house is me and I am it. My house is where I like
> to be and it looks like all my dreams.
> —*The Big Orange Splot* by Daniel Manus Pinkwater

Message from Carole Hyder:
In most alternative modalities—like taiqi, qigong, acupuncture, feng shui—the underpinning concept is that everything is energy. Any culture that has a strong connection to nature knows this to be true. Recently, science has come around to verifying the same idea that all matter is made up of energy. When further experimentation confirmed that someone observing a phenomenon can change the actual phenomenon, the definition that "everything is energy" expanded to incorporate thoughts as well.

We are all connected through this energy which makes us part of an entire network. Our actions and our thoughts will not only affect our immediate surroundings, they will also somehow impact the black bamboo plants growing on PoTu Shan Island off the coast of China. As remote as that may seem, it may also explain why some days we move through unexplained suffering and pain. We may be feeling the impact of a grieving mother in Boston. Why would a system like this be set up anyway? Why couldn't we simply deal with our own issues, keep them for ourselves, and let everyone else do likewise?

Well, we would be missing out on a very rewarding and inspiring potential.

Not only is there a connection between everything concrete and conceptual, but this connection has a consciousness of its own. Artists will share that in the midst of their creation, something happens and the artwork dictates their next move. My friend and mentor, Margaret, has indicated that when writing any fiction work, her characters, once developed, decide how the plot should unfold. The exhilaration of being part of a jam session with other musicians is that you get lifted out of the predictable progressions into something that no one expected. Something outside of ourselves intervenes to create a better experience, perhaps a more truthful one, but certainly a more exhilarating ride.

This interaction is not limited to artwork, novels and music, but is possible within your own home as well. There is a potential that exists in this spatial format that can open figurative doors, not just the literal ones. It is possible to establish a reciprocal rapport with your home in which you receive guidance and support, as well as discover an arena in which you can be who you truly are. Your home becomes your piece of music, the characters in your novel, your artwork—because, like all the other creative moments, it exemplifies the concept that "everything is energy."

By finding ways to connect with your home, you will be able to access the answers as well as the questions that lie within the walls. You may explore new possibilities for you and your home. You can create the life you always wanted and the life your home dreams about.